The Power of Resilience

The Power of Resilience

How Women Bounce Back from Crisis

Julia Baldwin, PhD

Foreword by Ed Baldwin

Vantage Press
New York

Published by Vantage Press, Inc.
419 Park Ave. South, New York, NY 10016

Manufactured in the United States of America

ISBN: 978-0-533-16355-7

Library of Congress Catalog Card No.: 2010922909

2 4 6 8 10 9 7 5 3 1

To the memory of my son, Andrew Brugal, R.I.P.,
and all the women who have achieved
resiliency in spite of significant
adversities, difficulties or oppositions.

Their perseverance is an inspiration,
and can remind us all of that
hope which exists for everyone,
with love, respect and admiration.

Contents

Acknowledgments

First and foremost, I would like to give all the honor and glory to my Lord Jesus Christ for working all things together for good in my life. Secondly, I am very grateful for the many people who contributed to the collaborative process of this work. To the memory of my resilient son Andrew Brugal R.I.P., your strength and kindness were truly Godly. You will forever be admired and adored! To my mom, Josefa, and my sister, Tiffany—after God, you have both been my fortresses and rock in this journey called life. To my father, Ralph, thank you for always supporting and believing in me. To my little brother Wesley, my most sincere gratitude for believing in my dreams and assisting me in raising Andrew. To my relentless brothers, Ed and Jimmy, thanks for always being so loving and supportive; your words of encouragement have kept me going in the worst of times. To my wonderful sisters-in-law, Marie, Beate and Xaviera, thanks for my gems Caitlin Marie, Jeremy, Chloe, Ella, Jaylen and Janae.

To my Sanctuary Ministries, Inc., flock, thank you for your endless prayers, confidence and support over the last eighteen years. To Mari and JD, thank you for all the encouragement and patience along the way; your insight, assistance, and confidence in me motivated me to get this book done. To Dr. Rafael Campo, Dr. Rafael Alfonzo, and Dr. Mark Dunbar, thank you for your medical care and support in keeping me healthy to achieve this milestone in my life.

Last but not least, special thanks and acknowledgment to all the research participants; without you this book would not have come to fruition.

Foreword

I have been privileged to witness resilience at its best in Julia and her son, Andrew Brugal. Numerous times, when we've embarked on conversations regarding resiliency, I related to their expressions of value and relevance, since they clearly reconcile with my own personal perspective on people and success. But interjecting these thoughts into a discussion relating to adversity — one of the most important subjects in human nature — is, to say the least, an unexpected topic of conversation among siblings. Being cognizant that resiliency is, for most people, probably one of the least understood topics, it has been a delightful surprise to become versed in this pinnacle truth.

Most individuals think of resilience as merely the quality of being perseverant. My observation, however, is that most of us respond to hardships and stressors with inner strength, instead of drawing on the vast array of influences (constituents) that contribute to the final product. Not only to coping strategies or interventions, specifically, but also to becoming successful and better people *after* the adversity than we were before. For example, as Dr. Baldwin suggests, there is also the need to learn more about the personal and familial origins of resilience, which may be biological, neurological, psychological, learned, or result from some combination of factors. There is also the misconception that if we've performed well — whatever "well" is, in our opinion — then we expect to rise to the top. If we haven't done so well, our expectation is reduced accordingly. In this sense, we live by outcomes rather than by resilience. Moreover, we are always challenging ourselves and one another to "try harder." We seem to believe that our success in life (however we define success) is basically up to us: our commitment, our discipline, and our zeal, with some help from God along the way.

People who become resilient and successful leaders have natural leadership qualities, while other people who don't have those qualities become excellent resilient individuals through training. But even naturally resilient leaders don't come ready-made; we all need a little work.

The economy, in recent years, has tested the resilience of many, from major institutions to world governments to the common person. With global financial markets on the brink of collapse, governments across the globe have proven that in times of despair they can find solutions and avoid collapse. Individuals who have lost their jobs, their homes, who have been broken spiritually, have found the resiliency to go on living. They have searched and found their inner strength to bounce back from total despair and find their way—one step at a time.

A resilient person is someone who is on top of things in his or her realm of influence. Yet it is amazing how many resilient individuals are not in positions that influence the lives of thousands. The relevant point is that we are *fulfilling our potential*: I am seeing my dreams and visions fulfilled. I don't believe this is just for a handful of people. I believe it is for all people to fulfill their potential, in spite of opposition, peril, and conflict in their lives. You, too, can rise to the top, snap back from your bad experiences, difficulties, privations, afflictions, calamities, unfortunate situations and negative circumstances, flourishing more triumphantly and victoriously than ever before.

This book, *The Power of Resilience: How Women Survive Crisis,* can set the foundation for you to be your very best, despite all the hardships that have occurred in your life! This book is about people and affect. It demonstrates the difference they can make in achieving ultimate success in life—not simply because of their situation and their commitment to success, but because of the impact all of us can make in the lives of those we have the opportunity to associate with and serve.

The message in the book is clear. *The Power of Resilience* has a responsibility to the ethical, professional, and personal development of every individual in becoming perseverant in the face of trials. The book is laid out in a simple, easy-to-follow format. The focus on resilience, people, and leadership responsibilities is reinforced with graphic examples of contemporary transformational, successful, high-profile women. Being from all levels and walks of life, these leaders, who live what they genuinely believe, enhance and optimize the potential in all individuals. In her characteristic style, Julia conveys the message that people, parents, doctors, actors, board directors, athletes, and politicians can, when faced with adversity and opposition, respond with personal determination, belief in self, faith, and hope.

This book treats all of us to a wonderful array of useful ideas on the significance of resilience and the recognition of leadership as a moral responsibility. It demonstrates the many ways in which people join together to experience the power of resilience.

Ed Baldwin
Director, Royal Bank of Canada (RBC)
Capital Markets Finance Division, New York

Chapter 1

Introduction

My interest in resiliency emerged due to various stressful events that occurred in my life. To name a few, when I was eight years old, my mother and two younger brothers and I left our homeland of the Dominican Republic to join my father, who had been in the United States for many years. As an immigrant to the United States, I experienced the harsh cruelty of mockery from other children as I underwent the process of assimilation and acculturation. Shortly after our arrival, I experienced emotional abandonment for the first time—my father decided to start a new family. As an adult I experienced abandonment by a husband in a city where I was alone with a nine-month-old baby, jobless, with no family or friends, and no support system. This abandonment eventually led to a divorce.

Five years after the divorce, I experienced a life-threatening illness when I was diagnosed with cancer. I was told that my disease was terminal, but I survived. Later, I enrolled in a seminary school, where most of the other students were male; most were not fond of women preachers or ministers, and I experienced a lot of criticism. However, I was successful and was later appointed to the position of senior pastor. The most recent challenge has been that of my once healthy and only child being diagnosed with renal disease and undergoing end-stage renal failure; he passed away on August 26, 2008.

Somehow I was able to snap back and rise above these adversities. I was able to psychologically have closure on the abandonment in my life; my parents have an incredible marriage of almost fifty years, and my dad is the most emotional, physical and psychological support system for me and the rest of my siblings. I was able to go back to school and graduate with honors in two master's programs (in counseling psychology and theology). I have also completed a PhD program in leadership and neuroscience with honors. In my career path, I was able to succeed in becoming the chief administrative officer for a well-known university. In terms of my health, I am in remission and have never felt better or healthier. As a senior pastor, I am responsible for a growing congregation with approximately seventy-five members. I was also very active in assisting my son in the process of resiliency throughout his education, kidney transplant, and cancer. I am still learning to live with the deep pain and anguish of the death of my only child.

I did not know how my strength developed to rise above disadvantages; this heightened my curiosity to investigate this by examining different studies and theories in the literature. I wanted to be able to contribute to others in the area of personal formation that is gained from undergoing a crisis and bouncing back after stress. Specifically, this refers not only to coping strategies or interventions, but also to becoming successful and better than before the adversity. I believe that it is of great importance to be able to identify and explain the factors that contributed to this resilience.

In my reading, I realized that there was a body of work that explained this phenomenon to a certain degree. However, I found that the literature identified several missing areas—for example, the need to learn more about the personal and familial origins of resilience, which may be biological, neurological, psychological, learned, or some combination of factors. Questions arose in my mind: Is resiliency something that can be learned? And is there a critical period for the development of resilience? My goal is to provide additional insights on this subject. Those who examine and study resilience as it develops across the lifespan and under different types of stressors may also gain insight into these questions. Responses to such questions will provide information and may ultimately influence how individuals, educators, doctors, parents, and organizational leaders work to foster the quality of resilience in others.

It is clear that this world needs leaders who are capable of challenging the status quo, of developing intricate professional networks, and of working within complex and changing conditions. As humans in this world, we all face increasing uncertainty, ambiguity, and change. This highly charged atmosphere can only remain ethical with the leadership talent of people who influence others from a foundational base of core values.

Transformational leadership offers the basis for a leadership paradigm built on moral and ethical underpinnings. Transformational leadership requires highly personal characteristics. One attribute deemed essential to successful transformational leadership is resiliency, yet this quality is seldom discussed in the leadership literature. The purpose of this book is to investigate the resiliency experiences of ten contemporary, transformational, successful women leaders. The leaders were asked how they experienced and applied resiliency in their lives, and the author identified resilient, transformational, successful women. For the purposes of this book, *resilient* refers to those who have had the capacity to bounce back and rise above disadvantage; *transformational leaders* are those who lead by moving beyond self-interest and, therefore, transform their followers into fully committed, mission-dedicated team members (Bass, 1990a; Bolman & Deal, 1992; Brooks et al., 1995; Burns, 1978a; Garmezy, 1991; Masten, Best, & Garmezy, 1990). This definition of resiliency is important in order to distinguish the construct from other phenomena, such as coping. Resiliency is not simply about "getting by" after a crisis occurs; it reflects a strength that is developed or manifested in light of a crisis (Valentine & Feinauer, 1993).

The study of resiliency in leadership is relatively new. Therefore, there is much to learn about resiliency theory and intervention strategies. As this topic is still a relatively new area of study in social science literature, the author's aim in this book is to provide insight and illumination as well as to impact the body of knowledge dedicated to the study of resilience. Further, the author hopes that the information gathered may provide approaches that can be used by educators, parents, doctors, and organizations to recognize and promote resiliency in others.

In the twenty-first century, organizations are dealing with increasing uncertainty, ambiguity, and change at unprecedented rates. This atmosphere requires the leadership talents of people who influence from core values. Leadership is obligated to convey tenets associated with moral and ethical behaviors. Transformational leadership offers the basis for such leadership and may be defined as

> occurring when one or more persons engage with others in such a way that leaders and followers raise one another to higher levels of motivation and morality. Their purposes, which may have started out as separate but related . . . become fused. Transforming leadership ultimately becomes moral in that it raises the level of human conduct and ethical aspiration of both leader and follower, and thus it has a transforming effect on both. (Burns, 1978b, p. 20)

In addition, transformational leadership is built on moral and ethical underpinnings and strives to motivate both the leader and follower, and at the same time is seen as raising the ethical and moral conduct of both (Bass, 1990b; Burns, 1978b). In addition,

Bass (1985) contends that transformational leaders align their own personal principles with those of the group, organization, and society. This notion suggests that transformational leaders operate primarily from a value-driven personal philosophy. What then constitutes this personal philosophy, and how is it internalized and operationalized?

Bass (1985) offered the first glimpse of an answer to the aforementioned questions. He asserts that possibilities such as "family values, strong mothers, absence of inner conflicts, role modeling, adult experiences, approaches to using power, ambitions, and ideals" (p. 293) may lead to an understanding of what contributes to being transformational in outlook and behavior. In addition, Avolio, Waldman, and Yammarino (1991) suggest that transformational leadership does not happen by chance. Certain preexisting conditions set the stage for the development of would-be transformational leaders. These authors posit that early role models and one's family, as well as non-family factors, help shape the self-confidence of the potential leader. Interestingly, the authors suggest that the interaction of events unique to individual development with events common to an entire population can affect the type of leader a person will become.

Underscoring the highly personal characteristics of transformational leaders is a need to understand how one develops an attribute deemed essential, resiliency, the oldest quality associated with leadership; yet this quality is seldom discussed. Slocum, Ragan, and Casey (2002) offers a consistent yet different perspective. He suggests that leaders are regularly faced with serious situations, and at times, even life and death issues, for their companies. At such times, resiliency may be very important.

Certain questions arise: How does resiliency develop, and how does resiliency contribute to the development of a transformational leader? In an attempt to further explore the attribute of resiliency, this book explored the following questions: (1) How do transformational women leaders who face difficulty, adversity, or opposition, experience resiliency and become successful? (2) What exactly is that quality of resilience that carries them through life? (Coutu, 2002) (3) How does resiliency work? (Coutu, 2002) (4) How do those who are resilient survive stressors to which the majority succumb? (Werner & Smith, 1992) (5) What are their perceptions of personal and spiritual growth as a component of leadership development? (Fox, 1994; Hawley, 1993; Senge, 1990) (6) What is the importance of these women knowing themselves well and understanding their personal motivations? (Bennis, 1998) and (7) Does having a mentor assist in the process of resiliency? (Koenig, 1997)

Resilience is a relatively new area of study in social science literature. In contrast to studying disease processes of mental health research, resiliency theory provides an alternative, nonpathogenic framework from which to examine how one survives the challenges of life, including but not limited to illness.

In contrast to coping, which reflects an individual's ability to negotiate the deleterious effects of a stressor or crisis, resiliency involves an individual's ability to become stronger, not in spite of, but rather because of the experience with the stressor. (Mosack, 2002, p. 4)

Resilience is viewed more as a process that develops over time than an attribute that is transmitted through genetic endowment. Rutter and Taylor (2002) posit that resilience is conceptualized as a composite of stress-resistant characteristics that include self-esteem, autonomy, a sense of personal competence fueled by the ability to take responsibility for one's actions, and a capacity to seek out and maintain fulfilling interpersonal relationships. Much of the research on resiliency has focused on the following elements: identifying demographic and personality characteristics of the stress-resistant individual (Garmezy, 1991a; Masten, Best & Garmezy, 1990; Luthar, 1991) linking intergenerational processes to adaptive or maladaptive functioning (Fonagy et al., 1994); describing the environmental origins of risk and adversity (Brooks-Gunn & Chase-Lansdale, 1991; Radke-Yarrow & Brown, 1993); and explaining how protective processes facilitate positive coping styles (Rutter, 1987). Even though these studies have generated an understanding of the crucial determinants of protective functioning, many questions remain about possible ways to promote resiliency and how individual differences combine with work and social factors as the catalyst for favorable leadership results. Simple main effects are not enough to explain the complex interplay of personal environment factors that influence the development of stress resistant capacities (Compas, Hinden, & Gerhardt, 1995).

The concept of resiliency may provide a means for identifying why some women leaders not only survive, but also succeed under stressful situations. Fostering women's leadership resiliency should be a priority if women leaders want to have a positive influence on other women and their communities. In fact, women who are not resilient will probably be dissatisfied, frustrated, and poor role models for other women (Koening, 1997).

Chapter 2

The Background to the Problem

It is generally agreed that the crisis of leadership is not limited to business; it is apparent that all facets of society are suffering. Families, hospitals, churches, schools, governments, private and public organizations are all faced with a pressing need for leadership. Now in the twenty-first century, leaders will become more important as organizations respond to the increasing diversity and ambiguity in institutions. Furthermore, Bolman and Deal (1992) make the point that there is a severe shortage of qualified people to lead corporations.

Leadership has been the focus of many books, studies, and scholarly endeavors; these include many different accounts of leadership styles. From trait theory to emerging paradigms, each school of thought has provided insight into the vast array of leader behaviors and attributes. Interestingly, no one school has been shown to be highly prescriptive for effective leadership. The construct of leadership is complicated and has many definitions. Rost (1995) notes there is no single commonly accepted definition of leadership; however, many leadership theorists agree that leadership is primarily about positive or negative influence (Bass, 1985; Bennis, 1994; Greenleaf, 1977; Luke, 1991; Northouse, 1997; Ramey, 1991; Yukl, 1994).

Leithwood and Duke (1998) support this ideological premise by asserting that leadership is what brings meaning to the collective actions of individuals. They also state that leaders need to take to heart the importance of creating a shared reality among those they lead. Bolman and Deal (1992) lend support for the releasing of potential. They contend that the "heart of leadership lies in the hearts of leaders. By connecting with one's spirit one can reclaim the enduring human capacity that gives our lives passion and purpose" (p. 106). The authors point out how individual efforts can accumulate into a shared reality. These collective positions suggest the importance of transformational leaders, especially in today's highly turbulent and chaotic environments. Inasmuch as transformational leaders apparently are needed, one is left to ponder the question of personal attributes. Does resiliency contribute to the success of transformational women leaders?

Over the years, many authors have written about attributes that enable one to be a successful leader. The list of attributes is long; however, the one that appears to offer hope for emerging leaders is resiliency. According to many authors, determination, an aspect of resiliency, is a foundation for transformational leadership (Bolman, 1995; Burns, 1978; Kouzes & Posner, 1995; Northouse, 1997; Tichy & Devanna, 1990). Resiliency gives the leader an ability to create a vision, challenge the process, and allow potential to unfold. Bass and Aviolo (1994) state that leadership is a process whereby one essential ingredient is resiliency. What appears to be missing from the leadership and leadership research is the idea of how resiliency works.

It is suggested that resiliency is a human quality rooted in a person's entire existence. Furthermore, it is asserted that resiliency is essential to self-affirmation, and the resilient person acts in accordance with a desire to reach higher levels of identity and actualization. Therefore, one can make the assumption that resilience stems from a person's sense of purpose and personal mission. Bass (1985) suggests that resiliency is a virtue upon which all virtues and values are established. This idea, coupled with Tillich's (1952) concepts, suggest a highly personal nature to resiliency. Bass and Aviolo (1994) offer resiliency as a process toward becoming. This personal, philosophical outlook reflects a critical balance of motivational certainties, which are formulated by the person's commitments. Therefore, these concepts suggest a greater need for people and women leaders in particular to understand resiliency theory and how this knowledge might assist them to rise above life's difficulties.

Due to the highly personal nature of resiliency, one limitation may be the possibility that findings are due to some other interpretation, such as dismantling of political and societal gendered barriers, instead of idiosyncratic factors of personal nature. Also, perhaps, the findings may be due to a developmental process associated with age and professional status.

This book will identify participants by selecting a purposeful sample with members chosen based on their transformational leadership style and their having displayed resiliency. Inasmuch as this book study attempted to describe the experiences of resiliency development in transformational, successful women leaders, it is by design a limited view of the experiences of a small, purposeful sample.

Questions arise when people study leadership. One question is what or who helps to create the difference between positive and negative effects of leadership. Burns (1978) asks how leaders are formed and if leaders and followers raise one another to higher levels of morality and motivation. He notes the purpose of these leaders is to raise the consciousness of their followers by appealing to moral values (Yukl, 1994). Burns and others have called this process transformational leadership.

Additionally, transformational leadership offers the most comprehensive and compelling argument for effective leadership. Bass (1990) suggests the following:

> Transformational leadership occurs when leaders broaden and elevate the interest of their employees, when they generate awareness and acceptance of the purposes and mission of the group, and when they stir their employees to look beyond their own self-interest for the good of the group. (p. 21)

This book of resilient, successful women leaders includes an in-depth discussion of the transformational leadership model (Bass, 1990; Burns, 1978) and Theory F (Forbes, 1993).

There are several assumptions involved in this book: (1) There is a process by which resilient, transformational, successful women leaders are developed. (2) Resilient, transformational, successful women leaders have their own resilient formation processes. (3) Resilient, transformational, successful women leaders have important contributions to make regarding their experiences of how resiliency may be promoted in others.

Chapter 3

Other Theories, Articles, and Research Books on Resiliency

Since the founding of the United States, women have slowly made great progress in achieving rights. The twentieth century witnessed the legal acknowledgment of many rights that had previously been denied to women. Until the latter half of the twentieth century, women were often denied liberties, and their spouses determined their worth. The twenty-first-century American woman is now usually defined by her own worth and accomplishments.

Forbes' (1993) Theory F Transformational Leadership Model, which acknowledges the feminine attributes of transformational leaders, provides one of the frameworks from which leadership is considered for this book.

Theory F

A narration of Forbes' (1993) Theory F Transformational Leadership Model is described by Githens (1996):

> Transformational Leaders lead from a foundation of values. They value the ethics of care, interdependence, empowerment, diversity, and social justice. Integrity, excellence, and authenticity are their hallmarks. These leaders are risk-takers and, in collaboration with colleagues, they achieve unparalleled results. They are

accountable. Transformational Leaders honor intuition and feelings, humor and celebration. They are comfortable with paradox, and ambiguity. Holistic in their outlook, these leaders attend to body, mind, emotion and spirit. Transformational Leaders exhibit both feminine and masculine characteristics. They vary their leadership styles to be effective. Finally, transformational leaders are self-aware, are constantly learning and define success in their own terms. (p. 7)

Githens (1996) added:

Reading this work brought awareness for the first time language that described some of the internal struggles I had experienced as a women leader in bureaucratic organizations. It validated my experience as similar to that of other women leaders. This awakening was like a breath of fresh air, or a weight off my shoulders. I no longer felt that I had to be just like my male counterparts in order to be successful. This awareness gave me permission to explore gender-related approaches to leadership. Specifically, it spurred me on to explore the issue of leadership from a feminine perspective. My aim became focused on trying to understand how women set about accomplishing their goals while remaining authentic to a genuinely feminine world-view. (p. 30)

Resiliency

According to a study by Blechman, Prinz, and Dumas (1995) on coping, competence, and aggression prevention, the resiliency phenomenon, so defined, applies across the life span to survivors of acute and chronic stressors and risk factors. These include, for example, children who avoid disruptions in adult work and family roles despite mentally ill parents; people who have experienced concentration camps, war zones, or impoverished households; and those who have observed community violence or endured sexual abuse. They might also include those who have experienced wars and rape survivors who avoid later posttraumatic stress disorder and substance abuse.

According to Block (1991), resilient survivors avoid adverse outcomes through ego resilience (resourceful, flexible responses to novel or stressful situations, as measured by the California Q-set). This helps decide whether children work through and grow beyond their difficulties. Longitudinal and cross-cultural studies reported by Blechman et al. (1995) have found that high ego resiliency ratings predict empathy, delay of gratification, reasoning, problem solving, IQ, and certain personality traits (Agreeableness, Extroversion, Conscientiousness, and Openness to experience). She also states that high ego resiliency ratings are associated with future avoidance of adverse outcomes such as substance abuse, but such correlational evidence cannot make a causal link between ego resilience and resilient survival. As Stroufe (1997) points out, it is important to avoid the temptation of circular reasoning, identifying people as resilient survivors simply because they score high on a paper-and-pencil measure of ego resilience.

Resilient survival of excessive stress is attributed by Block (1991), Garmezy (1993), and Werner and Smith (1992) to three factors: (1) personal characteristics (e.g., coping strategy, intelligence, physiological reactivity, temperament); (2) nuclear family characteristics (e.g., cohesiveness and structure; parents), and (3) extra-familial characteristics (e.g., community organization, mentoring, supportive school environment). Excessive stressors, such as homelessness, do not appear to have uniformly adverse effects; instead, protective factors moderate impact. Resilient survivors describe life-changing turning points when protection levels increase due to a caring mentor, supportive spouse, or religious conversion.

The definitions that have been used for resiliency similarly reflect this problem-absence focus. Blocker and Copeland (1994) note, "Resilient youth are exposed to high stress, but show few or no signs or impairment. Protective factors ameliorate distress, adversity and risk" (p. 288). Additionally, they purport that resiliency is found in those "who are exposed to high-stress, but show few or no signs of impairment" (p. 299). In a longitudinal study of children who developed prenatal complications and experienced adverse childrearing conditions, Werner (1984) defined resiliency as "the ability to recover from or adjust easily to misfortune or sustained life stress" (p. 68). The focus of resiliency in these cases seems to reflect one's ability to adjust or cope.

Resiliency has also been described as the ability to thrive despite deleterious or risky circumstances or experiences. Masten, Best, and Garmezy (1990) define resiliency as "a process, capacity, or outcome of successful adaptation despite challenges or threatening circumstances . . . good outcome despite high risk status, sustained competence under threat and recovery from trauma" (p. 426).

Similarly, Herrenkohl, Herrenkohl, and Egolf (1994) describe resilient individuals as those who are academically "high functioning" (p. 302). Another way of conceptualizing resiliency is that of "the positive pole of individual differences in people's response to stress and adversity" (Rutter, 1987, p. 316). These theorists seem to be identifying a construct that is very different from simply coping with a tragedy or loss.

Beardslee (1989) discusses three reviewed studies in which a strong connection was demonstrated between self-understanding and resilience. Resilience is defined as unusually good adaptation in the face of severe stress. In-depth initial and follow-up interviews were carried out. Subjects of the three studies were civil rights workers in the South, survivors of childhood cancer, and adolescents whose parents had serious affective disorders. Self-understanding appears to be associated with adequate and realistic cognitive appraisal, action with thought, change over time, and protection from effects of stress. Self-understanding appears to be an important inner psychological process in resilient people. This concept is limited because it does not address the issue of how much understanding is present in those perceived as nonresilient individuals.

According to Masten et al. (1990), in a study of the protective role of competence indicators in children at risk, four types of competence emerge as significant predictors: work, social, interpersonal, and cognitive competence. Measurement parameters related to resources, stressors, and vulnerability or protective factors are highlighted. Competency has been linked to feelings of well-being. Coping is aimed ultimately at retaining competence.

Rutter and Taylor (2002) explore various conceptual considerations of resiliency. They describes it as a changing characteristic. Resilience results from repeated incidents of successful coping with stressors, not from avoidance. Therefore, different sources of measurement must be repeated over time. There should be a focus on risk mechanisms (e.g., processes that affect one child in a family may not affect the family). People's own actions can shape environments and create risk situations. There are certain times in people's lives when they will turn to more adaptive approaches. Resilience can be fostered by interventions that make individuals effective in planning and shaping what happens to them.

Coutu (2002) states that theories abound about what makes resilience. According to her research, she observed that almost all the theories overlap in three ways. Resilient people possess three characteristics:

> A staunch acceptance of reality; a deep belief, often buttressed by strongly held values, that life is meaningful; and an uncanny ability to improvise. One can bounce back from hardship with just one or two of these qualities, but you will only be truly resilient with all three. These three characteristics hold true for resilient organizations as well. (p. 48)

According to Dean Becker, president and CEO of Adaptiv Learning Systems, a company in Pennsylvania that develops programs about resilience training, "More than education, more than experience, more than training, a person's level of resilience will determine who succeeds and who fails. That's true in the cancer ward, it's true in the Olympics, and it's true in the boardroom" (Coutu, 2002, p. 47).

McCubbin, McCubbin, and Thompson (1992) discuss the processes that promote family endurance, coping, and survival. Research on the impact of war on American families was conducted over four decades. Family appraisal is of central importance to family adjustment to stress, leading to the family's ability to move from major catastrophe to a shared opportunity. Then a solid foundation for changes in family coping and functioning develops. Ethnicity and culture play a critical role in shaping a family schema. For example, social networks and social support are traditional values in Asian, Black, and Hispanic groups. Assuming responsibility for the care of elders or the chronically ill was found to be a family expectation across certain ethnic groups.

In another study, by Garmezy (1993), the current status of resiliency research is summarized. By definition, he states that resiliency has an elastic quality; it is described as the ability to bend under stress and then rebound. Effects of cumulated stress can be negative, and resilience can diminish over time. The protective triad—easy temperament, supportive family, and social support systems—is explained. Factors that affect protection will be found in the person, families, and communities. Poor children possess a potential for achievement that should be tapped. He posits that if family cohesion, children's adaptation, and the usefulness of community support are components of family resilience, then the problem of poverty should be a part of the national political agenda. Government financial support should be available for interventions that bolster resiliency.

Egeland, Carlson, and Stroufe (1999) examine resiliency using original data from a seventeen-year study of children and families living in poverty. The effects of poverty are cumulative. Resilience is conceived as a capacity that develops over time. An organizational-developmental perspective is taken placing emphasis on meaningful patterns of behavior, not specific outcomes. Factors related to resilience are identified as emotionally responsive care giving, early competence, organized home environment, child capacities of intelligence and language, and low overall level of risk. These findings served as a guide for the development of a preventive intervention program for high-risk parents of small children.

Ramsey and Blieszner (1999) share their personal, diverse, and complementary life experiences in pastoral counseling and academic teaching and researching the task of conducting research and reporting findings in a way that balances science and spirituality. This book explores the voices of women over the age of sixty-five during the mid-1990s, all members of the Lutheran denomination, who live in two locations: southwest Virginia and northwest Germany. Participants shared their perspectives on life and spirituality.

These women developed strength to bounce back from life's adversities, oppositions, or difficulties. They exhibited resilience and strong spiritual faith "in spite of" or "because of" the challenges, struggles, and problems they encountered, ranging from war to deaths of children, parents, siblings, and spouses; to deteriorating health, including blindness for one; to loneliness and fear; and to financial poverty.

The researchers suggest that participants exhibited resiliency because of their abilities to intertwine thinking and feeling about the past, present, and future; their abilities to relate to people and God personally and with a sound theology; and their abilities to look to a future that goes beyond the present life.

Krovetz (1999) states that emotional resiliency is one of the key features of successful leaders. He believes that schools and education can make a difference in students' lives, and he discusses what he believes is good practice from different parts of the United States and from different school cultures. He shows some examples of good educational practice that emerged from the work of the schools he studied. The research is culturally and at times linguistically bound, but there is a global message of not giving up on students.

McCubbin, Thompson, and Futrell (1998) examine the strengths and resources of African American families in their quest to understand resiliency. Their book emphasizes the role of culture in the families' development of positive coping strategies and reveals the resiliency of African American families in overcoming disadvantages in ordinary family life. The book is organized in two parts: Families and Communities and Family Relationships. The chapters, written by various authors, provide up-to-date qualitative and quantitative research on neglected topics such as the levels of satisfaction in African American marriages, perceptions of fatherhood among African American adolescents, healing forces in African American families, and African American military families.

One of the most important points of the study is that to build African American families, it is crucial to view problems as interrelated. Further, problems of law enforcement, health care, and housing must be addressed in order to strengthen families.

McCubbin et al. (1998) suggest that the study of resiliency in minority families also involves confronting racism and exploring mutuality or "a bi-directional movement of feelings, thoughts and activity between persons" (p. 813). They emphasize that resiliency in African American families is especially significant, given the structural changes in society such as the shift of United States jobs overseas, the transformation of industrial jobs to service occupations, and the transitions in state and federal welfare laws.

Successful Women Leaders

In large American corporations, even though women comprise almost 50% of the workforce and over 30% of management, fewer than 5% of senior managers are reported to be women (Powell, 1998). However, successful senior executive women have developed strategies, skills, and leadership styles to overcome challenges and barriers throughout different phases of their careers. Many complex factors contribute to executive women achieving senior positions.

A study by Powell (1998) explored how senior executive women cope with difficult situations, perceive challenges, and overcome barriers, identifying some of the factors that facilitated their advancement to senior executive positions. The study described internal barriers, including self-confidence and personality traits, and external barriers, including gender biases and the "old boys' network." This qualitative, descriptive study consisted of interviews with twelve senior executive women located on the East Coast of the United States. Participants described their perceived experiences, skills, coping styles, and self-concepts. The key findings in this study included: (1) the complex way senior executive women developed and maintained self-confidence as well as educational and professional support systems; (2) their approaches to meeting challenges and overcoming barriers within the corporate culture; and (3) the way they developed their leadership styles and the skills needed to cope with difficult situations. The participants of this study were action oriented; they gathered required resources, and they acquired education to achieve their positions.

Another study, by Walker (1993), investigated the meaning of personal success for a group of women who came to middle age in the second half of the twentieth century. What do women need to know to feel successful in adult life? What can young people learn from older women? This interpretive study was based on the analysis of 244 letters written over a twenty-four-year period by eighteen women identified as leaders and academic achievers during their college years. Text analysis was used to understand the concept of success and make meaning out of the women's personal struggles to achieve. The middle-class women provided insight into the meaning of success and achievement for those who value personal time, family life, career advancement, and community involvement.

The study identified six themes that were found in the letters and were fundamental to the feelings of personal success for the women: (1) valuing connection and continuity in relationships, (2) balancing care and responsibility, (3) working to make a difference, (4) abandoning a search for closure, (5) embracing life's defining moments, and (6) finding space and models of success. The findings suggested important concepts for young people making career and life decisions.

Cormier's (1997) study investigated how five women in the early 1990s became leaders of various provincial political parties throughout the Maritime region of Canada. Although liberal feminists gained optimism from the success of these women, questions arose as to whether their gains were truly a sign of change in a patriarchal society. Did the rise and prominence of these particular women mean greater participation and success for other women in the future? Cormier argues that these women were successful not because of the dismantling of political and societal gendered barriers, but rather because of personal considerations (financial security, child care responsibilities, household duties, etc.). This thesis illustrates that class, location, and personal circumstances were only partial factors in the success of the five women.

A study by Koenig (1997) investigated the perceptions of women leaders regarding their career successes and identified the benefits to women of having a mentor. A random sample of one hundred individuals was selected from the members of the Alumnae Association of Leadership Texas from 1983 to 1995. As a group, the respondents perceived themselves to be quite successful. Seventy percent of this group had been mentored, and 70% of mentors were male. Two-thirds of this group felt that their mentors made important contributions to their career successes. The findings of this study suggest that leadership programs need to teach women the importance of mentoring and how to mentor. The author notes that as more women advance to higher career positions, perhaps more will be available to serve as mentors for other aspiring women. According to Curtis (2002), less than 1% of the one thousand largest companies in the United States have women CEOs. However, Curtis notes that in the nation's community college system, women have made considerable progress in occupying leadership positions. About one-quarter of the two-year, postsecondary institutions in the U.S. have women presidents. This varies from state to state. For example, in North Carolina, only 15% of the community college presidents are women; in Massachusetts, one-third of such schools have a woman president. Furthermore, Curtis states that female leaders are inclined to talk more about mentoring future leaders, male and female, within their organizations. Female leaders have a greater propensity to encourage others to enter the "administrative pipeline," thereby ensuring the succession of institutional leadership (p. 2).

The Contribution of this Book

The importance of this book can be viewed within four distinct areas. First, this book may add supplementary information to the body of knowledge about leadership attributes. The current literature defines numerous attributes of successful, transformational leaders. The list of attributes is long; however, the one that appears to offer hope for emerging leaders is resiliency.

Second, this study may provide a basis for understanding how transformational leaders develop resiliency. Resiliency is viewed as an affirmation of oneself (Tillich, 1952); Duke (1998) states that resiliency is a virtue upon which all others are built. Third, since

research on resiliency is still in its infancy, and there is much to contribute to resiliency theory and intervention strategies, this book may
add to the body of knowledge dedicated to resiliency.

Fourth, the information gathered from this study may suggest approaches that can be utilized by educators, parents, doctors, and organizations to promote resiliency in others. Therefore,
this study is important because it seeks to provide answers to
questions regarding resiliency in successful leaders and the possibility of resiliency being promoted in others.

Chapter 4

Successful Women Leaders

History provides examples of resilient, successful, transformational women. This section presents a brief portrait of the lives of four such leaders—Susan Brownell Anthony, Harriet Tubman, Eleanor Roosevelt, and Eva de Perón—to provide a framework within which to further examine resilient, successful, transformational women leaders today. The above-mentioned, successful women leaders are certainly not the only ones who might have been selected. However, their lives align with the definition of resiliency in transformational, successful women leaders as those who have had the capacity to bounce back and rise above disad vantage and who led in relationships that moved beyond self-interest and transformed their followers into fully committed, mission-dedicated team members.

Susan B. Anthony. Susan B. Anthony was born in Rochester, New York, on February 15, 1820, and attended the Friends' Boarding School in Philadelphia (1837–38). After teaching at several academies and heading the Female Department of the Canajoharie, New York, Academy (1846–49), she retired from teaching to contribute her time to the temperance movement in Rochester. While a delegate to the 1852 Sons of Temperance meeting in Albany, she was discriminated against because of her sex; afterward, she organized the Woman's State Temperance Society of New York. She also served on the committee for the American Anti-Slavery Society (1856–61) and was active in teachers' organizations, urging equal pay for women teachers. She worked for the passage of the New York law of 1860 that gave women equal property rights. During the Civil War, she organized the Women's National Loyal League, which worked for the emancipation of Blacks (Garraty & Sterstein, 1974; Moritz, 1989). After the war, she focused her energy on the women's suffrage movement. She urged an addition to the Fourteenth Amendment that would guarantee women the right to vote. She also published a women's rights periodical, *The Revolution.* Together with her lifelong associate Elizabeth Cady Stanton, she organized the National Women's Suffrage Association in 1869, serving as chair of its executive committee. In collaboration with Stanton and other feminists, Anthony compiled and edited *The History of Women's Suffrage* (four volumes, 1881–1902). Anthony made a significant contribution to the quest for equal rights for women (Garraty, 1974; Moritz, 1989).

Harriet Tubman. Harriet Tubman was born Harriet Ross in Dorchester City, Maryland, around the year 1821. Because she was born into slavery, her exact date of birth is unknown. She worked as a field hand on a large Maryland plantation and received no education. She was forced to marry John Tubman in 1849, but they separated soon after. When it appeared that she would be sold in the South, she escaped to Philadelphia and became active in the Underground Railroad, working as a cook to raise money to assist fugitives. In 1857, she rescued her parents and settled them in Auburn, New York. Tubman was an outspoken abolitionist and an advocate of women's rights, discussing these subjects during her journeys throughout the United States (Garraty & Sterstein, 1974; Josselson & Lieblich, 1993; Moritz, 1989).

Tubman worked with the Union army in South Carolina during the Civil War as a laundress, cook, and nurse. Additionally, she acted as a scout for Union soldiers and a spy behind Confederate lines. She was an activist who rescued and led slaves into the free states and Canada. Since her work was under cover, many details were lost. Nevertheless, it is believed she assisted with two or three hundred slave rescues. These rescues undoubtedly inspired other runaways (Garraty & Sterstein, 1974; Josselson & Lieblich, 1993; Moritz, 1989).

Eleanor Roosevelt. Eleanor Anna Roosevelt was born in New York City, on October 11, 1884. She was the niece of Theodore Roosevelt and was raised by her grandmother and educated in private schools in the U.S. and abroad. She married her fifth cousin, Franklin D. Roosevelt (FDR), in 1905. During the Progressive Era, she was a supporter of social reform who also fought for the rights of minorities and was active in numerous consumer, welfare, and charity programs. Roosevelt was active in the women's division of the Democratic State Committee in New York. In 1930, she helped her husband campaign successfully in the state gubernatorial elections; two years later she campaigned with him for the presidency (Garraty & Sterstein, 1974; Josselson & Lieblich, 1993; Moritz, 1989; Roth, 1949).

Eleanor Roosevelt became the most active First Lady in the nation's history after her husband's election. She traveled over 40,000 miles during one year seeking to win sympathy for New Deal programs; and she also worked with many reform organizations, especially the NAACP. Later, she became assistant director of the Office of Civilian Defense when the United States entered World War II. She often visited American soldiers in the southwest Pacific and the Caribbean (Garraty & Sterstein, 1974; Josselson & Lieblich, 1993; Moritz, 1989; Roth, 1949).

Eleanor Roosevelt accepted an appointment as United States delegate to the United Nations after the death of FDR in 1945. She also served as the chair of the UN Commission on Human Rights, where she helped draft a universal Declaration of Human Rights. Eleanor Roosevelt was a leader of women's movements and was one who promoted social justice and civil liberties (Garraty & Sterstein, 1974; Josselson & Lieblich, 1993; Moritz, 1989; Roth, 1949).

Eva de Perón. Eva de Perón was born Maria Eva Duarte in 1919 in Los Toldos, a village of Buenos Aires province, Argentina. Her family moved to a larger town after her father's death, and they operated a boarding house in this town. After attending high school there for two years, Duarte went to Buenos Aires in order to become an actress (Garraty & Sterstein, 1974; Josselson & Lieblich, 1993; Moritz, 1989).

Duarte met Colonel Juan Domingo Perón, an undersecretary in the Argentine Ministry of War, shortly after. One of her earliest political interests was the organization of an industry-wide radio workers union. In October 1945, Juan Perón married Eva Duarte. Immediately afterward, she participated in her husband's campaign for the presidency of Argentina, certainly an unprecedented action for an Argentinean woman of that time. One aspect of the campaign managed by Perón was the radio broadcasts. She directed her appeals chiefly to the less privileged groups of Argentina's population, whom she addressed as *los descamisados,* or the "the shirtless" (Garraty & Sterstein, 1974; Josselson & Lieblich, 1993; Moritz, 1989).

During her husband's presidency, she administered a personal welfare program, distributing food, medicine, and money. These social programs, as well as her frequent appeals for national women's suffrage in Argentina, created opposition from the upper and middle classes and support from underprivileged classes (Garraty & Sterstein, 1974; Josselson & Lieblich, 1993; Moritz, 1989).

Chapter 5

Anna Escobedo Cabral

Anna Escobedo Cabral served as the forty-second Treasurer of the United States from January 19, 2005 to January 20, 2009. She was the next highest-ranking Latina in the Bush administration (after the resignation of Rosario Martin). Prior to this, Cabral headed the Hispanic Association on Corporate Responsibility (HACR) as president and CEO. HACR, a nonprofit organization headquartered in Washington, D.C., is a coalition of the largest and most influential national Hispanic organizations in the United States. Its mission is to ensure the inclusion of Hispanics in corporate America at a level commensurate with the Hispanic community's economic contributions. To this end, HACR has established partnerships with thirty of the nation's most prominent corporations to measure Hispanic inclusion in four core areas: employment, procurement, philanthropy, and governance.

Prior to joining HACR, Cabral served as Deputy Staff Director for the U.S. Senate Judiciary Committee, one of the most powerful and productive committees on Capitol Hill. The Committee's jurisdiction ranges from oversight of the Department of Justice and the nation's criminal and drug enforcement laws to approving federal judicial nominations; it includes review of immigration, antitrust, patents and trademark, and technology-related legislation. In addition, she simultaneously served as Executive Staff Director of the U.S. Senate Republican Conference Task Force on Hispanic Affairs.

Cabral majored in political science at the University of California, Davis. After, she'd earned a master's degree in public administration from the John F. Kennedy School of Government at Harvard University, President George W. Bush appointed Cabral to the Council on the 21st Century Workforce in April 2002.

Question #1: Please discuss some of the adversities, difficulties, or oppositions you have experienced in your life/career.

All of the resilient, transformational, successful women leaders discussed numerous adversities, difficulties, and oppositions they experienced in their lives or careers. They described life issues and discrimination issues. They also recounted how they believed they kept focused.

Poverty and Family Difficulties

Anna Escobedo Cabral talked of several issues. She discussed living part of her life in extreme poverty. She noted,

> We'd turn to every possible government source for— to, you know, we lived off of welfare, butter and cheese lines, bought our clothes from a second-hand store with a voucher given to us by the church, where you go in and pick up a handful of underwear and a pair of shoes, one dress, one pair of slacks. . . . and then I worked. I was the oldest of five children, so I worked after school. I cleaned people's houses, and I got an after-school job through the government. There was a federal government program, and I kept doing that after my father put his business together, so he and I together were able to probably raise $250 a month and with that $250 support a family of seven.

Furthermore, Cabral discussed the difficulties involved because of her mother's suicide attempt, saying,

> She decided to attempt suicide, and it wasn't that—today I can understand it, and I can even talk about it, but for many, many years I couldn't, and to live through all of that, and then to have your parents say that—she wasn't really saying that—but to basically decide that you as a child were not important enough to hang in there, to be there for. I don't know why, but probably one of the most difficult things I ever lived through; I mean the food didn't matter, and the job didn't matter, and the house didn't matter. You know, losing the house didn't matter. Not having anything to eat didn't matter, but when my mother made a decision to leave the, you know, this earth, and I took it personally. I was affronted by that, and for a long time, though I tried really hard to understand her, I had a hard time doing so, and what had been an absolutely fabulous mother-daughter relationship ended almost within minutes.

Question #2: What kept you focused?

Family

Another way that interviewees noted they keep focused is because of their families. For example, Anna Escobedo Cabral said the reason she is so strong is because of her parents, particularly her mother:

> My mother is probably the reason I am so strong even though she may not want to—she may not really realize that—and I thought about this, that interesting sort of development, you know, that by doing what she did, she gave me a strength that she will not understand. . . . My mother I think is probably responsible for my

being able to survive every single one of the things that God has decided I should experience and learn from, so it's been kind of interesting.

She continued regarding her parents:

[They had] some difficult cultural traditions that make life a little more complicated, and you know, I'm proud of both of them for being able to find a way to get around all of that, live through it, and find ways to support one another outside of those traditional trappings, and really make a wonderful life for each other, and set an example of love that was incredible. I mean, they loved each other very, very much, and that I think was a tremendous gift that I could never, ever repay anyone for.

Education

Anna Escobedo Cabral also observed that education is a guiding force in her ability to remain focused:

I started to dream about other things that were possible, and I started to get angry about the fact that so many of the kids in the neighborhoods where I had grown up didn't have that kind of opportunity, and decided that that was what my life would be about. Finding ways to make sure that it wasn't an accident that would guarantee that you had access, but rather that those opportunities would open up. So that's what I decided to do with my education

Work/Responsibility

Several interviewees pointed out that their work and/or a sense of responsibility helped to keep them focused. For example, Anna Escobedo Cabral said:

I felt like everything was my responsibility. I had to make sure everything kept—was kept together—and it was perhaps my mother's illness, and a whole range of other things, and the fact that my father relied so much on me . . .

Question #3: How would you define resiliency?

In discussing definitions of resiliency, the interviewees talked about having the ability to bounce back or snap back, being able to accept adversity or hardship, looking to the future, and refusing to be a victim.

Refusing to be a Victim/Looking to the Future

Anna Escobedo Cabral explained that she believes resiliency is about looking toward tomorrow:

I would say it is the ability to keep ever present the knowledge that the sun will rise tomorrow. Some people have compared me to Scarlett O'Hara, but I honestly believe—and I don't take that as an insult, by the way—that unless you learn and can live by that philosophy, I think that the world will pull you down and suck you in. There are very, very difficult times, and I have recalled when I've gotten up and could not, as bright as the sun was shining, could not see it. You know, it was staring me in the face, and I was so sad and so beat, but in my mind, I told myself that it was still out there, and that if I could just get through the day, tomorrow would be better, and eventually there was a tomorrow that was better. And you just have to sort of hang on to that belief, or that expectation, and get through the day that you are living.

Question #4: How does/how has resiliency work(ed) for you? In other words, what made you persevere and not give up?

In discussing how resiliency has worked for them, the interviewees talked about God and faith, personal determination, and meeting the expectations of others.

Personal Determination

Anna Escobedo Cabral indicated that her determination arises from her conversations with herself, self-counseling. She explained:

> What works for me is when I am having a very, very, very difficult time or I'm being challenged, I begin to literally be my best counselor. I talk to myself. I talk to myself constantly, and whenever something bad pops in my head, and I say it sometimes out loud, mostly out loud . . . I figure, Anna, you can do this. You have to hang on. You have to do—you know, there's X, Y, and Z. Don't worry about this. Tomorrow's another day. The sun will shine, and I literally have that conversation with myself, and I counsel myself. . . . and if it requires 24 hours of talking to myself, it's 24 hours I give it. Whatever it requires, I do that. . . . And in some ways [I am] creating a new reality; creating one that will get you through the next few minutes or the next few hours or the next few days, reminding you what's important so that—because you can't really call a friend and expect them to counsel you 24 hours a day. You know, they would do everything they possibly could, but they're not there when you're all by yourself in the middle of the night, and so you can be there for yourself. So that's what I've done, and it works.

Question #5: Do you have a belief regarding how resilient women survive stressors to which many succumb? Please explain.

While discussing their beliefs about how resilient women survive stressors, the interviewees mentioned life experiences, trust in God and hope, and belief in oneself and others.

Belief in Oneself and Others

Several interviewees observed that they are able to survive because of their belief in the self and/or family support. Anna Escobedo Cabral noted that external support is important:

> I think a lot of it has to do with what's happening internally and what kind of external support you have. I think it would make a world of difference to a woman who's in a place where she's facing a very difficult situation if she has no help, whether she's her own best friend, or she has somebody else she can turn to. I think women who can find support from someone else can make it back, and what we need is to find ways in which they can reach out.

Question #6: How is personal growth related to your leadership success?

When discussing the relationship between personal growth and leadership, the interviewees focused on facilitating the work of others and learning from experiences. (Bennis, 1998)

Learning from experiences

Cabral observes how she owes it to various negative experiences that developed drive and perseverance in her:

I think there's something inside that drives or doesn't drive, and I believe it is in all of us, but somebody can wake it up. Somebody can snap it into place, and whether it's you who snaps it into place or somebody else, for example, that little thing about the teacher who yelled at me when I was tiny and told me I was stupid. I could have either decided I will be stupid or I could be the defiant eight-year-old who says, "I'll show you I'm not stupid."

Question #7: How is spiritual growth related to your leadership success?

When discussing how spiritual growth is related to leadership success, Anna Escobedo Cabral commented:

I use prayer daily, and it's not something I talk about. It's not something you do for show. It's not something—it's just the way that I live. I talk to Him 24 hours a day. . . . And through God . . . and spiritualism for me is particularly important. It is not something I wear on my cuff, but it's something I live in a way that is very, very much a personal experience for me, that guides everything I do.

Question #8: Discuss your own personal motivations and influence on your ability to transform your followers.

While examining the concept of personal motivation and transforming followers, the interviewees talked about following God's path as well as placing the focus on others through modeling, learning, listening, and assisting.

Placing the Focus on Others Through Modeling

Anna Escobedo Cabral commented that others look to her for direction:

> I do know in the position that I hold and in the positions that I've held that people look to you for direction. They look to you for support. They look to you for confirmation. They look to you for ideas, and you just have to be in a position to be able to provide some of that. I honestly believe that people will rise to any level of expectations, and that when you lead, it's really more helping people find where they fit and helping them to meet this set of expectations, and helping them find their own strength because I think—I really believe in more of a consensus approach, and a team approach than anything else, probably maybe because I'm female. ... I don't believe that a leader is the person that stands up and gives orders . . .

Anna Escobedo Cabral discussed the value of finding ways to support others and of shared success:

> I find a way to give back to a community and create opportunities for a community of people who don't deserve anything less and that in and of itself drives you to succeed, and then you say if I'm going to do this, this is not a one-person mission. This is a mission that other people believe in, that you have to share, that you have to move toward together, and whatever you're doing there's a place where everybody sits and everybody can contribute, and leadership is just finding that place where everybody sits so that we can succeed together.

Question #9: Did you have a mentor throughout the difficult times in your life/career? If so please discuss the benefits you received by having this mentor.

Nine of the interviewees said they had mentors throughout the difficult times in their lives or careers. In regard to this question, the interviewees discussed family and friends as well as spiritual guidance. Interviewees also explained the benefits of having mentors.

Family and Friends

Several interviewees discussed the importance of family mentors. Anna Escobedo Cabral stated that her mother gave her "strength she will never understand." She also included her grandparents and her great-grandparents as great mentors. Additionally, she stated that her high school algebra teacher and a friend in college were her mentors through difficult times.

Benefits

Eight interviewees answered this part of the question. Anna Escobedo Cabral and Rose Tydus both mentioned that the benefits they received were that their mentors were always there for them.

Question #10: Do you know other resilient, successful, transformational women who might contribute to and participate in this research study? Please describe this individual or individuals.

When asked for names of other resilient, successful, transformational women leaders, the interviewees mentioned women from

several areas. These areas included religion and education, politics and business, and family members and friends.

Family Members and Friends

Anna Escobedo Cabral suggested Antonia Coello Novello, M.D., a friend from college who "has faith, confidence and perseverance." And the Surgeon General of the U.S. from 1990 to 1993.

Chapter 6

Kristen Hughes

Kristen Hughes is a dedicated educator committed to working collaboratively with community partners and a self-motivated professional with proven leadership skills. Within a multicultural, ethnically diverse community, she has served as the Superintendent of Schools for the Archdiocese of Miami since 1997.

From 1992 until 1997, Hughes was an elementary school principal for the Archdiocese; she improved instruction, increased enrollment, and supervised faculty and staff at Our Lady Queen of Martyrs Elementary School in Fort Lauderdale, Florida, and Holy Family Elementary School in North Miami, Florida. From 1974 until 1997, she worked as a teacher, department chairperson, and curriculum writer for public and private elementary, secondary, and postsecondary schools.

Hughes has certification as a paralegal from Barry University and a master's of science degree from Florida International University. She has also completed her graduate studies at Nova University School of Law.

She is a member of various professional organizations and has also served on many committees. She serves on the Florida Catholic Conference Accreditation Committee, the Miami-Dade County School Health Advisory Board, the Holy Cross Hospital Medical Advisory Board, the Broward County Schools Medical Heath Advisory Board, the Broward County Public Schools Title

VI Advisory Committee, the National Catholic Educational Association, the Florida Association of Academic Non-Public Schools, the Southern Association of Colleges and Schools, and the Principals Advisory Council for the Archdiocese of Miami.

Question #1: Please discuss some of the adversities, difficulties, or oppositions you have experienced in your life/career.

All of the resilient, transformational, successful women leaders discussed numerous adversities, difficulties, and oppositions they experienced in their lives or careers. They described life issues and discrimination issues. They also recounted how they believed they kept focused.

Family Difficulties

Kristen Hughes noted a family difficulty she experienced. She felt deprived of a sense of roots because her family moved so often:

> Our family moved quite a bit; by the time I came to ninth grade here in South Florida, we had moved 14 different times; I had been in 13 different elementary schools. I think it was, at the time. . . . It was a wonderful thing in some ways to always be the new kid, the new girl at school. But also that sort of longing to have roots that were real permanent. But again, that's the way I grew up.

Question #2: What kept you focused?

Kristen Hughes also discussed her family, noting the importance of her son, parents, sisters, and brother. She said:

I think, my son being older now, he's still a focus in my life. I divorced his father when he was three years old. ... [I was] pretty much alone with that child most of his life. So that focus was a good focus to have initially, to make sure that he was clothed, fed, schooled, happy, whatever that might have been. And of course, I have a very supportive family, I have my mother and father who are still living, thank God; I have sisters and a brother. ... I think we've all encouraged one another.

Question #3: How would you define resiliency?

In discussing definitions of resiliency, the interviewees talked about having the ability to bounce back or snap back, being able to accept adversity or hardship, looking to the future, and refusing to be a victim.

Kristen Hughes used imagery to describe the "bouncing" process. She said:

Okay, you know, I think, I keep thinking about those commercials where they step on the grass or the carpet and it bounces back up, you know just that, even when you're getting squished, even when you've got the heavy load on top of you, that you just bounce back up somehow, that you, you know, the wool fibers or whatever, whatever twitchy things there are in you spring back up. That's how I look at resiliency.

Question #4: How does/how has resiliency work(ed) for you? In other words, what made you persevere and not give up?

In discussing how resiliency has worked for them, the interviewees talked about God and faith, personal determination, and meeting the expectations of others.

Meeting the Expectations of Others

Other interviewees indicated that they have been resilient because they needed to help others or meet the expectations of others.

As an example, Kristen Hughes discussed how she wanted her family to be proud of her, and she did not want them to be disappointed:

> I think just the expectation. Whether it was said or not from my parents, from my maternal grandmother as well, who was a very, very strong woman, who had overcome so many problems in her lifetime. I think just seeing her, knowing her, and knowing that I wanted her to be proud of me; I wanted my family to be proud of me even when there were . . . dozens and dozens of reasons why I could be sitting in my bedroom, you know, sucking my thumb, twirling my hair for lack of a better thought, that, you know, it was kind of like, nope, I'm not going to let this get me down. I will get up, I will brush my hair, and I will go out and do what I need to do. So, but I do think again, whether it was example, whether it was expectation, or some combination in there that really did force me, or I forced myself to think that someone would be disappointed, someone would be upset if I didn't become resilient and didn't fight back.

Question #5: Do you have a belief regarding how resilient women survive stressors to which many succumb? Please explain.

While discussing their beliefs about how resilient women survive stressors, the interviewees mentioned life experiences, trust in God and hope, and belief in oneself and others.

Kristen Hughes noted that those who survive make no excuses for themselves:

> I think that society makes it very easy for people to fail and very easy to make excuses. . . . I think that a lot of excuses are made for people, and I think we make excuses for ourselves. And my feeling is that somehow the women that I've watched who survive adversity, who go through problems, whether it's a relative, whether it's other women that I've watched or learned from, somehow they just cut to the chase . . . and it's just, you just keep going. You keep your nose focused north, or whichever direction you're going, and you keep walking. And I guess that's as close to a belief system as I have.

Question #6: How is personal growth related to your leadership success?

When discussing the relationship between personal growth and leadership, the interviewees focused on facilitating the work of others and learning from experiences.

Kristen Hughes discussed the importance of change in facilitating personal growth:

> That's the toughest one [question] so far. I think, I've sort of gone kicking and screaming into certain growth phases, and I think I have been forced to grow. And, sometimes it was very difficult and sometimes I really didn't want to. And I know I cling to the familiar. Change is difficult. . . . I am a very resistant person and a very stubborn human being, and I think that stubbornness can be a real asset, and it also can be a little, you know, it can definitely be a detriment to growing,

so sometimes I go kicking and screaming to change
and grow, and I realize that about myself. And then
I wrestle with the thought of whatever it is I have to
change . . . and truly anybody who's been in a classroom or has had their own child, they know. You can
fight with two-year-olds till you're dead, and they're
not going to change. You as the adult, you as the
teacher, the leader, you're the one that has to change.
And I'm a little resistant to change, sometimes, a lot of
the time, but I realize how important it is, and I think
I can, I know I have been able to foster that for people
that I have worked with in a leadership position.

Question #7: How is spiritual growth related to your leadership success?

Kristen Hughes also commented about how church beliefs have
influenced her:

> I do think having been raised with church as an impor-
> tant part of my life from earliest memory on, being a
> Catholic, being part of, in Catholic schools for quite a bit
> of my schooling, and again just that whole idea of God
> accepting you the way that you are, God wanting you to
> be the very best person that you can be, and help the
> other people around you be the best that they can be.
> Again, I don't always put into practice as well as I could,
> but I do think that as I have grown spiritually, I have been
> able to realize that especially the core of church, that
> spirit of hope, and love, and care, and compassion, the
> more you let in, the more people you love, the more peo-
> ple you care about, the larger circle of love that really
> does envelop you, the larger sense of spirituality, I think
> that really can make a huge difference with folks . . .

Question #8: Discuss your own personal motivations and influence on your ability to transform your followers.

While examining the concept of personal motivation and trans-forming followers, the interviewees talked about following God's path as well as placing the focus on others through modeling, learning, listening, and assisting.

Still other interviewees noted the importance of assisting and serving others. Kristen Hughes mentioned the value of pro-viding guidance:

> I think, I guess again being the oldest child, I guess I was always leading somebody and I didn't realize it for a really, really long time. . . . Somehow I inspire people to be confident in what they are doing. They trust me to take care of what they need to have done for them or completed for them, or the guidance they need . . .

Question #9: Did you have a mentor throughout the difficult times in your life/career? If so please discuss the benefits you received by having this mentor.

Nine of the interviewees said they had mentors throughout the diffi-cult times in their lives or careers. In regard to this question, the interviewees discussed family and friends as well as spiritual guid-ance. Interviewees also explained the benefits of having mentors.

Family and Friends

Several interviewees discussed the importance of family mentors.
Kristen Hughes stated that her maternal grandmother was a kind of "quiet sort, the cheerleader, a demanding sort of cheerleader."

She also named her mother as a mentor. Additionally, Kristen Hughes said mentors have been a "good mirror for everybody in the family to reflect" what they wanted or needed.

Question #10: Do you know other resilient, successful, transformational women who might contribute to and participate in this study? Please describe this individual or individuals.

When asked for names of other resilient, successful, transformational women leaders, the interviewees mentioned women from several areas. These areas included religion and education, politics and business, and family members and friends.

Hughes Mentioned:

> I am thinking about a woman who works here in this office with me, and she is again very resilient. She has been a teacher and principal now. She is a very private sort of person, but we've been friends for about twenty years.

Chapter 7

Claire Mignon

Claire Mignon was born in Haiti; she now lives in Miami, Florida, with her son and her dog. She truly enjoys her profession as a pharmacist. Pharmacy is the profession concerned with the preparation, distribution, and use of drugs, once called apothecaries. Mignon mentioned that there was a time pharmacists compounded their own medicines, but today, pharmaceutical manufacturers supply most drugs. Pharmacists must still compound some medicines and be able to prepare antiseptic solutions, ointments, and other common remedies. She enjoys advising people about how to select nonprescription drugs.

Mignon's training and career in pharmacy were not easy. As a pharmacy student in Haiti, she took courses in the biological sciences, chemistry, and mathematics, as well as in the humanities, to receive her bachelor's degree in pharmacy. She also completed specialized professional courses. These courses included pharmacology, the study of the effects of drugs on living things; pharmaceutics, the physical chemistry of drugs; and clinical pharmacy, the application of the pharmaceutical sciences to patient care. However, in the United States a pharmacist must graduate from an accredited college of pharmacy. After finishing this five- or six-year program, graduates must complete one year of internship under the supervision of a practicing pharmacist. Mignon received her bachelor's degree in pharmacy from the University of Medicine and Pharmacy in Haiti and received an equivalency in the United States sixteen years later from the Foreign Pharmacy Graduate Certification Program. In 1996, she completed an equivalency of the Foreign Pharmacy Graduate Equivalency Certification (FPGEC). She received her pharmacy license in Miami, Florida, in 1998.

Mignon is the President and Executive Director of Hand of God Ministries, Inc., a Miami–based nonprofit organization that is responsive to the health needs of low-income communities. Hand of God Outreach, Inc., is part of the ministries, providing screening, and training health management, community needs assessment, and health education. In addition to the screening for diabetes, blood pressure, and cholesterol, the health clinic emphasizes the use of medications to prevent their interactions and enforces compliance. The clinic also provides moral support, counseling, job training, and education.

Mignon is also a proud member of the American Pharmaceutical Association, which is the national organization of pharmacists in the United States. The association seeks to maintain high standards of practice among its members. She is a member of the DCPA (Dade County Pharmacy Association), the NCPA (National Community Pharmacy Association), and the Florida Association of Pharmacy. She is also a member of the Realtor Association—she has been a Realtor since 1990—and a member of the National Association of Female Executives (NAFE).

Question #1: Please discuss some of the adversities, difficulties, or oppositions you have experienced in your life/career.

All of the resilient, transformational, successful women leaders discussed numerous adversities, difficulties, and oppositions they experienced in their lives or careers. They described life issues and discrimination issues. They also recounted how they believed they kept focused.

Family Difficulties

Several of the interviewees discussed life issues related to family difficulties. For example, Claire Mignon related that her marriage was one of abuse. She stated:

> My husband was a very successful man, and he was a well-known man; he had a lot of fans and a lot of women after him. He was the kind of man that women would go after him; he did not need to go after them. He started beating me up all the time. Every Friday I would get beaten for no reason at all . . .

Question #2: What kept you focused?

How She Kept Focused During and After Adversity

God and Spirituality

Several interviewees pointed out that God and/or their spirituality helped to keep them focused.

Claire Mignon gave a similar response, adding that hope together with trust in God helps her to keep focused:

> It was my trust in God, and the second thing was hope. Hope because throughout those moments God gave me some little sign—by word, by dream, by things that I saw—that there was a tomorrow. What kept me going was knowing that there was a tomorrow, whatever was going on, there was a better tomorrow. That kept me going, but also what kept me going was that I said, well, one day, one day, one day, and every day was one day, because that day will be coming. I did not know when, but that kept me going.

Question #3: How would you define resiliency?

In discussing definitions of resiliency, the interviewees talked about having the ability to bounce back or snap back, being able to accept adversity or hardship, looking to the future, and refusing to be a victim.

Resistance

Claire Mignon defined resiliency as the ability someone has to resist the hardships of life and for that individual to find a way to go on and not be crushed.

Question #4: How does/how has resiliency work(ed) for you? In other words, what made you persevere and not give up?

In discussing how resiliency has worked for them, the interviewees talked about God and faith, personal determination, and meeting the expectations of others.

Personal Determination

Several interviewees discussed their resiliency in light of personal strength and determination. For example, Claire Mignon told a story of the importance of never giving up. She said:

> One day at a time, like if you survive today, that means you can survive tomorrow. All it takes is don't let your hand give up on whatever you are hanging on to. I always have the following as a picture in my mind. There was one time in my country when there was a hurricane that came with a lot of water and the water was so high, the water was as high as the top of a palm tree. . . . All the houses, everything was covered by water. . . . The people, when they came near a tree,

they would hang on to that tree. . . . People would come in boats to pick up those people who were hanging on to those trees. . . . But the water was coming with strength, and it was hard to hang on for long, and your arms would get tired, and you would want to give up. There was one person . . . at one point he could not hang anymore . . . and he just slipped away. . . . And that picture never left my mind, and the boat just came a minute after, and it was too late. So don't give up.

Question #5: Do you have a belief regarding how resilient women survive stressors to which many succumb? Please explain.

While discussing their beliefs about how resilient women survive stressors, the interviewees mentioned life experiences, trust in God and hope, and belief in oneself and others.

Claire Mignon discussed the value of hope in surviving stressors and noted some people give up because of a lack of hope:

> I think most of them give up because they don't have hope; I think hope is the number one because if I know there is a tomorrow that means that if I have a little strength, I can hang in there and get to that tomorrow thing. But if you don't have hope for tomorrow, and you don't know if tomorrow has something better, then you see something, you see yourself in the pit today, and you think tomorrow will be worse.

Question #6: How is personal growth related to your leadership success?

When discussing the relationship between personal growth and leadership, the interviewees focused on facilitating the work of others and learning from experiences.

Life Experiences

Claire Mignon mentioned:

> Well, how can I describe that [growth], when I got to
> fifty years old, people usually say that you are at the
> top of the hill. I celebrated that fifty birthday, because,
> I said, I am at the top of that hill and I am still going
> up! [Everything I went through] in those past fifty
> years is what has given me [knowledge]. I went
> through it step by step, and every time I went through
> a hardship, it made me stronger for the next one.

Question #7: How is spiritual growth related to your leadership success?

God, Divine Guidance, and Prayer

Several interviewees related that God and/or divine guidance is an
important part of their lives. For example, Claire Mignon said:

> Without God I would not be able to do anything, he is
> my Father . . . how do you say it . . . he is that ship's
> captain. And throughout my life, I don't take the credit.
> I always say God did it. Not me; God did everything
> for me.

Question #8: Discuss your own personal motivations and influence on your ability to transform your followers.

While examining the concept of personal motivation and transforming followers, the interviewees talked about following God's

path as well as placing the focus on others through modeling, learning, listening, and assisting.

Placing the Focus on Others Through Modeling, Learning, Listening, and Assisting

Two interviewees pointed out that they sometimes model and provide direction for others. Claire Mignon observed that others see and then follow her actions:

> Practically, people just look up to me. Those that know what I have gone through, they just see how I go through life and the positives in my life and they admire this, and they try to model it. . . . [They say] if she can do it, I can do it too.

Question #9: Did you have a mentor throughout the difficult times in your life/career? If so please discuss the benefits you received by having this mentor.

Nine of the interviewees said they had mentors throughout the difficult times in their lives or careers. In regard to this question, the interviewees discussed family and friends as well as spiritual guidance. Interviewees also explained the benefits of having mentors.

Spiritual Guidance

Three of the interviewees mentioned spiritual guides as mentors. Claire Mignon commented that she considers the Holy Spirit her mentor. She said discernment and prompting from the Holy Spirit have been beneficial.

Question #10: Do you know other resilient, successful, transformational women who might contribute to and participate in this study? Please describe this individual or individuals.

When asked for names of other resilient, successful, transformational women leaders, the interviewees mentioned women from several areas. These areas included religion and education, politics and business, and family members and friends.

Family Members and Friends

Claire Mignon mentioned Josephine Carde, who is a Christian single mother and an engineer who has had many hardships in her life.

Chapter 8

Janet Reno

Janet Reno was born in Miami, Florida. Her early life and career provide understanding of why she is such a remarkable person. Reno's father came to the United States from Denmark, and for forty-three years was a police reporter for the *Miami Herald*. Her mother raised four children and then became an investigative reporter for the *Miami News*. Reno is a compelling attorney and the first woman to serve as a state attorney of Florida. She majored in chemistry at Cornell University and became President of the Women's Self-Government Association.

In 1960, Reno enrolled at Harvard Law School, one of only sixteen women in a class of more than five hundred students. She received her LLB from Harvard three years later. Despite her Harvard degree, she had difficulty obtaining work as a lawyer because she was a woman. Ten years later, she was named Staff Director for the Judiciary Committee of the Florida House of Representatives, where she helped revise the Florida court system. In 1973, she accepted a position with the Dade County State Attorney's Office. She left there in 1976 to become a partner in a private law firm that years previously had denied her employment because of her gender.

In 1978, Reno was appointed State Attorney General for Miami-Dade County, Florida. She was returned to office by the voters four times. She helped reform the juvenile justice system, pursued delinquent fathers for child support payments, and established the Miami Drug Court. In nominating Reno to become the nation's 78th Attorney General, President Bill Clinton emphasized her integrity, saying, "She has demonstrated throughout her career a commitment to principles that I want to see enshrined in the Justice Department: no one is above the law." Reno was sworn into the office of the United States Attorney General on March 12, 1993. She served until 2001, making her not only the first appointed female, but also the longest-serving attorney general in the twentieth century.

Question #1: Please discuss some of the adversities, difficulties, or oppositions you have experienced in your life/career.

All of the resilient, transformational, successful women leaders discussed numerous adversities, difficulties, and oppositions they experienced in their lives or careers. They described life issues and discrimination issues. They also recounted how they believed they kept focused.

Job Opposition

One interviewee discussed the life issue of on-the-job problems. Janet Reno discussed her time as State Attorney of Florida and later as Attorney General:

> For 15 years as State Attorney, I had to handle large caseloads under very difficult circumstances, and there were crises relating to the McDuffy riots and other situations that I dealt with. As Attorney General, I dealt with the issue of Waco and the independent council,

and the Oklahoma City bombing, and the Elian
Gonzalez case, amongst others.

Gender

Two interviewees discussed opposition they experienced because
they are women. As an example, Janet Reno said:

> The first opposition I experienced was when my
> mother told me I couldn't go to law school. The second
> is when I tried to get a summer job between my second
> and third year of law school; a major Miami law firm
> would not give me a job because I was a woman;
> 14 years later they made me a partner.

Question #2: What kept you focused?

How She Kept Focused During and After Adversity

Work and Responsibility

Janet Reno noted that in order to remain focused:

> I just pursued what I thought was right. I tried to be as
> prepared as I could. I tried to make the right decisions
> based on what was the right thing to do. And then
> I tried to learn from my experience.

Question #3: How would you define resiliency?

In discussing definitions of resiliency, the interviewees talked
about having the ability to bounce back or snap back, being able to
accept adversity or hardship, looking to the future, and refusing to
be a victim.

Reno defined resiliency as the ability to bounce back or snap back.

Question #4: How does/how has resiliency work(ed) for you? In other words, what made you persevere and not give up?

In discussing how resiliency has worked for them, the interviewees talked about God and faith, personal determination, and meeting the expectations of others.

Meeting the Expectations of Others

Janet Reno noted that she meets the expectations of others by trying to do the right thing. She added, "I tried to ask all the questions, tried to make the best decisions I could, and then I accepted responsibility for them."

Question #5: Do you have a belief regarding how resilient women survive stressors to which many succumb? Please explain.

While discussing their beliefs about how resilient women survive stressors, the interviewees mentioned life experiences, trust in God and hope, and belief in oneself and others.

Making the Right Decision

Janet Reno mentioned that:

> Trying to make the right decisions allowed me to persevere and not give up under any of these circumstances.

Question #6: How is personal growth related to your leadership success?

When discussing the relationship between personal growth and leadership, the interviewees focused on facilitating the work of others and learning from experiences.

Facilitating the Work of Others

Janet Reno explained that personal growth is important in leading people to do their best. She said:

> Well, personal growth is important in leadership success. If you don't grow personally, you're not going to be much of a leader. [Personal attributes include] perception, guidance, understanding of other people, trying to do everything I can to make the people working with me able to have the capacity to do their best. A basic trust in people.

Question #7: How is spiritual growth related to your leadership success?

Janet Reno stated, "I think my belief in God, my confidence in God . . ." She also remembered that her "Presbyterian grandmother taught me that God helps those who help themselves."

Question #8: Discuss your own personal motivations and influence on your ability to transform your followers.

While examining the concept of personal motivation and transforming followers, the interviewees talked about following God's path as well as placing the focus on others through modeling, learning, listening, and assisting.

Janet Reno emphasized the importance of serving others through a commitment to using the law to protect the citizens:

> What motivates me is, I enjoy public service. I think it's the greatest undertaking a lawyer can pursue to try to use the law the right way to make America safer and freer and to give more people equal opportunity. My commitment to the law comes in the need to see it developed as a sword, a shield, a problem solver, and a peacemaker, and to try to use it in all those forms.

Question #9: Did you have a mentor throughout the difficult times in your life/career? If so please discuss the benefits you received by having this mentor.

Nine of the interviewees said they had mentors throughout the difficult times in their lives or careers. In regard to this question, the interviewees discussed family and friends as well as spiritual guidance. Interviewees also explained the benefits of having mentors.

Family and Friends

Several interviewees discussed the importance of family mentors. Janet Reno mentioned her mother, her father, various teachers along the way, and friends, as mentors. She said her mentors gave her good guidance, great wisdom, and strong support.

Question #10: Do you know other resilient, successful, transformational women who might contribute to and participate in this study? Please describe this individual or individuals.

When asked for names of other resilient, successful, transformational women leaders, the interviewees mentioned women from several areas. These areas included religion and education, politics and business, and family members and friends.

Politics and Business

Janet Reno mentioned Commissioner Katy Sorenson, who is a County Commissioner in Miami-Dade County.

Chapter 9

Marcy Roban

Marcy Roban is a metaphysician, author, mystic, visionary, spiritual educator, and holistic healer. She has dedicated her life to the transformation of human consciousness and to personal healing at the deepest level of being—the soul. Through this, she has inspired many on their path to greater self-understanding, fulfillment, healing, and awakening to their bio-spiritual nature.

Her education in this field has been nontraditional and developed from a lifelong curiosity about the nature of reality. This led her to receive great wisdom from her nonphysical spiritual guides, ascended beings of Light—"Spirit." During her twenty-year apprenticeship, they taught her many of the fundamental "whys" of things (the study of metaphysics), which answered and surpassed many of her lifelong questions about the following: the laws that govern creation; the grounds, limits, and criteria of human knowledge; the bio-spiritual epidemiology of disease; the holistic healing modalities; the "past-present-future"; and the holographic principles of reality.

It is these gifts of love that she is inspired to convey to her audiences. She uniquely presents an inspirational and provocative overview of personal growth, of spiritual (not religious) evolution, and of the parts people play in this growth through their thoughts, emotions, and actions—as well as the cellular consequences, and thus health consequences. Her delivery is simple and personal—the experience is profound and expansive.

The focus of Roban's body of work is to bring greater wholeness to the individual and therefore to societies, cultures, religions, and races; to facilitate alignment with the spiritual life and with the invisible teachers who guide people; to bring a more expanded perspective of metaphysical causation into the effects of daily lives; to help people free themselves from struggle and pain; to bring about greater peace within individuals, which translates into greater planetary peace; and to help evolve the concept of healing into a new paradigm.

She has been invited to speak at educational institutions and international organizations, and has appeared in the media more than forty times, reaching many millions with messages of inspiration and understanding.

In her recent book *Your Electric Self—A Self-Healing Manual,* she presents the layperson with an easy-to-read explanation of the interrelationship between the soul, the function of the mind, the feeling of emotion, and the creation of disease. It also offers the relevance these matters have to the circumstances in people's lives. This integrational approach to life and healing is one that Roban calls "Spiritual Science."

Roban was born in Havana, Cuba, and came to the United States at the age of four. She then made her home in Washington, D.C., and now resides in Miami, Florida. She is an ordained minister and a certified hypnotherapist. Her ministry is interdenominational and focuses on oneness, not differences. She is founder of the One World Movement—an international effort bringing together organizations whose focus is healing and uplifting people and the planet.

Question #1: Please discuss some of the adversities, difficulties, or oppositions you have experienced in your life/career.

All of the resilient, transformational, successful women leaders discussed numerous adversities, difficulties, and oppositions they experienced in their lives or careers. They described life issues and discrimination issues. They also recounted how they believed they kept focused.

Rejection

Mary Roban observed that rejection and judgmental attitudes were her biggest adversities, oppositions and difficulties. Roban said:

> Yes. I am a Hispanic woman. I arrived in this country from Cuba when I was four years old. From a very young age I was a very, very sensitive child, and started to develop abilities that were considered psychic or paranormal, and from that time until today many people think that this is very strange. [Thus], I've been very harshly judged when in fact it has become my life work, and not being psychic, but in fact feeling in the realm of metaphysics and spirituality. That has allowed me to connect to a far greater paradigm, to a more expansive version of reality than the ones we normally hold in our three-dimensional existences, and being that, that makes me a little bit different. I would say I've been rejected by friends, family and strangers alike.

Question #2: What kept you focused?

Marcy Roban observed that she receives divine guidance to help her through times of adversity. She explained:

> I have experienced such blessings in terms of knowing that I am always supported—always, no matter what happens. I read the signs, the energetic signs, and— which is in fact what I would consider—what I would

say to be in my terminology, in terms of my work, the handrails that we are given by divine guidance in terms of where to go and what to do, and how to act, and so forth and so on. That has helped me tremendously to move through adversity, and I have also come to the realization that all adversity is there to teach us something, and to make us stronger and wiser, and that, of course, is a personal choice. Because we could either go down into the vortex or swirl out of it, and go to higher dimensions, or higher realms or higher perspectives.

Question #3: How would you define resiliency?

In discussing definitions of resiliency, the interviewees talked about having the ability to bounce back or snap back, being able to accept adversity or hardship, looking to the future, and refusing to be a victim.

Being Able to Accept Adversity or Hardship

Two interviewees remarked that resiliency is about accepting and learning from adversity. Marcy Roban stated that resiliency is "the ability to accept adversity as part of life, and to step through it and beyond it with courage and determination and trust." Similarly, Claire Mignon had remarked that resiliency is "the ability somebody has to resist the hardship of life and a way to go around it and not let it crush you."

Question #4: How does/how has resiliency work(ed) for you? In other words, what made you persevere and not give up?

In discussing how resiliency has worked for them, the interviewees talked about God and faith, personal determination, and meeting the expectations of others.

Meeting the Expectations of Others

Marcy Roban commented that her courage comes from a desire to help others, saying:

> I do humbly consider myself a courageous person, and there is something within me that drives me, and that drive has always been to uplift, to heal, or to better myself, society, and those whose lives I touch in my work, and that propels me. It's something innate that always motivates me to move forward because I know that we're all here to help one another and to teach one another, and as I have learned from others, I also help others to learn.

Question #5: Do you have a belief regarding how resilient women survive stressors to which many succumb? Please explain.

While discussing their beliefs about how resilient women survive stressors, the interviewees mentioned life experiences, trust in God and hope, and belief in oneself and others.

Life Experiences

Marcy Roban also pointed out the value of the experiences and the energy of each life as a determinant of survival:

> All things are energetic, and because your soul is energy, there is a mathematics, there is a physics to each person's life, and not everyone's energetic [force] is the same frequency. So this leads us to realize that not only is everyone different, but everyone is different for a reason, and the way the mathematics of the culture, the family structure, and belief systems, the experiences that we have,

the religion that we are, the race that we are, are all components of that mathematics.Therefore, how each person
responds in a given situation depends upon those factors,
and some people have that mathematics which propels
them forward, and others get stuck in the experience that
they have ...

Similarly, Marcy Roban talked of finding a new perspective
through God:

It's a matter of finding those things which raise us
out and grasp on, and then move forward ... and you
are aligning to something greater than yourself, which is
what we call God, and that raises our frequency,
allows us to see a new perspective. It gives us courage.
It gives us impetus, and we move forward with greater
momentum.

Question #6: How is personal growth related to your leadership success?

When discussing the relationship between personal growth and
leadership, the interviewees focused on facilitating the work of
others and learning from experiences.

Learning from Experiences

Several interviewees mentioned how they learn from experiences,
thus growing personally. Marcy Roban talked of the importance
of learning though experience:

It is necessary for us to take every experience, whether
it's a relationship or whether it's an occurrence, or

whether it's in a society, in the world, on any level, but mostly personal, to say, "Okay. What is this teaching me? Where is this causing growth in my life? Is it helping me to let go of things I'm attached to?"

Question #7: How is spiritual growth related to your leadership success?

Marcy Roban related that spiritual growth has led her to a belief in a divine order:

> Spiritual growth is not only related to my success, but in my opinion it's related . . . to knowing that there is a reason for this madness, that there is a cause and an effect factor, and that there is divine guidance in all things. What becomes the joy in living as well as our pain in living is trying to figure out that puzzle, and it's literally a puzzle. And you take the pieces one by one and put them in place, and as you grow, the perspective expands, and you get to see the whole picture eventually, with time and experience, or as much of the picture as one can see while in an experience. So for me, my spiritual growth has been my life. . . . When I awoke to greater realities and to the fact that there is a rhyme and reason for life, and that there is divine guidance, and that all things are, in fact, in perfect order whether we like it or not, and whether we see it that way or not, has allowed me to, if you will, succeed in my work, to reach more and more people to make these truths available to them in order for their lives to become richer, fuller, with less trouble.

Question #8: Discuss your own personal motivations and influence on your ability to transform your followers.

While examining the concept of personal motivation and transforming followers, the interviewees talked about following God's path as well as placing the focus on others through modeling, learning, listening, and assisting.

Marcy Roban wants to assist others' transformation through knowledge of themselves and prevention of illness:

> My most fulfilled moments in my life are when I see transformation occur in people. . . . As far as what I do, I help people to integrate their four primary energy systems, and these are their spirit; their mind—that is their core beliefs; their emotions—emotional responses that are in their everyday lives; and their physicality, which means how they create illness, how certain things manifest in their body. And all four of those are energy systems. They actually interface, and there is a cause and effect, if you will, for any manifestation of illness, and any manifestation in your life, and so that's what the joy in my work is, is figuring that out, which is the fundamental why, and in my private practice, I help people in that way, whether it's an individual, or a couple, or a family, or someone that comes with an illness.

Question #9: Did you have a mentor throughout the difficult times in your life/career? If so please discuss the benefits you received by having this mentor.

Nine of the interviewees said they had mentors throughout the difficult times in their lives or careers. In regard to this question, the interviewees discussed family and friends as well as spiritual guidance. Interviewees also explained the benefits of having mentors.

Spiritual Guidance

Three of the interviewees mentioned spiritual guides as mentors. "My spirit guides, they are my mentors," commented Marcy Roban. She professed that spirit guides lead her in her actions.

Question #10: Do you know other resilient, successful, transformational women who might contribute to and participate in this study? Please describe this individual or individuals.

When asked for names of other resilient, successful, transformational women leaders, the interviewees mentioned women from several areas. These areas included religion and education, politics and business, and family members and friends. Marcy Roban named Barbara Mark Hubbard.

Chapter 10

Maria T. Sanjuan

Maria T. Sanjuan is Vice President for AXA Advisors. She has been associated with AXA Advisors, LLC (formerly Equitable Life) since 1975. She became a certified financial planner in 1988. Her outstanding sales accomplishments earned her a place as the first Hispanic in Equitable's prestigious Hall of Fame. She is also a qualifying and life member of the Million Dollar Round Table, the industry's top organization. Sanjuan's expertise in financial services and insurance has earned her a reputation for professionalism and success. She has been featured on television's *Good Morning America*, FFN, Miami, Florida Channel 10's *Here's to South Florida*, as well as on several radio talk shows and in newspaper articles. In 1998, she was awarded the National Builders Trophy by placing nationally among AXA regional vice presidents.

Sanjuan has been a resident of Broward County, Florida, for forty-one years. A strong belief in community service guides her personal and professional life. Her involvement with civic, professional, and philanthropic organizations is extensive. She is a founding member of the Boys and Girls Club of Hollywood, the Latin Chamber of Commerce, Hispanic Unity of Florida, the Coalition of Hispanic American Women–Broward Chapter, and the South Florida Chapter of the Women in Insurance and Financial Services.

She is a member of many organizations, including NAIFA, the Financial Planners Association, and the Broward Women's Alliance. She currently serves on the board of the Latin Chamber

of Commerce, Hispanic Unity of Florida, United Way of Broward
County, Broward Workforce One, Broward Financial Planning
Association Board, the Board of Community Solutions, and
Hollywood Medical Center. She is a trustee of the Fort Lauderdale
Chamber of Commerce. She is Vice Chair of the National
Conference for Community and Justice (NCCJ). She was reap-
pointed to the Florida Commission on Community Service in
2000. She currently serves on the Board of Governors for the
Museum of Art.

In 1998, Sanjuan received the World of People Award. The
March of Dimes also recognized her with a Women of Distinction
award in 1998. In 2000, the NCCJ and the Charles White Spirit of
Excellence Award of the *Miami Herald* presented her with the
Silver Medallion Award. She received the VISTA award again
from NAWBO in 2001, as well as the Liberty Award from the
Broward County Bar Association in May 2001. She was inducted
into Broward County's Women Hall of Fame in March 2002. In
April 2002, she received *Sun Sentinel's* Publisher's Community
Service Award, along with a $10,000 award to benefit the chari-
ties of her choice.

Question #1: Please discuss some of the adversities, difficulties, or oppositions you have experienced in your life/career.

All of the resilient, transformational, successful women leaders
discussed numerous adversities, difficulties, and oppositions they
experienced in their lives or careers. They described life issues
and discrimination issues. They also recounted how they believed
they kept focused.

Family Difficulties

Maria Sanjuan discussed her grandmother's suicide attempt:

I remember being like five and a half, the day she came over to live with us; I remember distinctly she tried to commit suicide and take some pills, and you know, you're saying, "What in the world is going on? You know, what have I done, you know, to—what have I done to this lady? What is going to be so bad going forward that, you know, she wanted to commit suicide?"

Sanjuan commented about the difficulties revolving around the death of her husband:

And he died three years ago of cancer, and that's all right. He's in a better place. No more suffering, you know, it was funny because, you know, it was horrible? I knew he was going to die because he smoked like a chimney. . . . It's a very challenging disease, as you know. It's a horrible thing because one day you're fine and you have a little hope, and the next day you're dying. . . . I did everything that I could humanly do, and I had told him that, you know, although the marriage wasn't the greatest at the end because of a lot of things . . . I told him, "I will be with you until I close your eyes."

Regarding the difficulty of her mother's death, she said:

And then my mother really started, you know, getting weaker, and it was horrible at the end with her. It was very trying, her death. She was a woman who was always afraid of dying . . . and it was hard . . . because at the end they get like little kids. . . . It was very hard for her to leave.

Sanjuan talked of another family difficulty—growing up without a father and helping to raise her siblings, saying:

I think that the most difficult thing in my life very early
on was to not have grown up with a father by my side.
My grandmother and my mother raised me and my two
siblings, a brother and a sister, and I'm the oldest of the
three, and I guess that—I guess that I took on being the
protector of my other—of my younger siblings, protector in many ways.

Discrimination Issues: Minority Problems/Gender

Maria Sanjuan experienced difficulties regarding language.
She stated:

> I came over here, and you know, the next big episode
> is not having anybody, not having anything, and being
> in a different country, and I always spoke English and
> all that, but you know, the funny thing is Americans
> spoke very fast, so I couldn't understand a word that
> they were saying . . .

Question #2: What kept you focused?

Work and Responsibility

Maria Sanjuan discussed how her work keeps her focused. She
noted, "My mother always taught me to be competitive, and I had
a great work ethic. I love to work. . . ."

Question #3: How would you define resiliency?

In discussing definitions of resiliency, the interviewees talked
about having the ability to bounce back or snap back, being able
to accept adversity or hardship, looking to the future, and refusing to be a victim.

Refusing to be a Victim and Looking to the Future

Maria Sanjuan defined resiliency as not being a victim. As she heard someone say, "In order to be a victim you have to give permission to somebody to victimize you." She added, "I think that's how you summarize what resiliency is."

Question #4: How does/how has resiliency work(ed) for you? In other words, what made you persevere and not give up?

In discussing how resiliency has worked for them, the interviewees talked about God and faith, personal determination, and meeting the expectations of others.

Personal Determination

Maria Sanjuan explained how her personal determination made her persevere and not give up:

> I think, you know, after you have touched bottom, the only way is back up, and with the same intensity in my life that I touched bottom, I wanted to surface again and not give up and go back! I look back now, and I realize that after being on Valium and wanting to die, there is absolutely nothing, nothing worth dying for except your children.

Question #5: Do you have a belief regarding how resilient women survive stressors to which many succumb? Please explain.

While discussing their beliefs about how resilient women survive stressors, the interviewees mentioned life experiences, trust in God and hope, and belief in oneself and others.

Belief in Oneself and Others

Other interviewees discussed qualities of the self such as commitment, self-image, and not making any excuses in order to keep going. For example, Maria Sanjuan said:

> You call it resiliency, but I call it competitiveness. I call it commitment. I call it being positive, looking at the bright side, and I am never thinking that I am better than anybody, that I am entitled to anything that is different from what life is all about.

Question #6: How is personal growth related to your leadership success?

When discussing the relationship between personal growth and leadership, the interviewees focused on facilitating the work of others and learning from experiences.

Breaking Traditions

San Juan described how relevant personal growth is related to her leadership success by not sticking to traditions:

> There is always a conflict between mother and daughter, and I always told my mother, "whatever you and Grandma instilled in me, I'm not going to do to my kids," so it was funny that I skipped a generation. I tried doing everything differently in raising my kids, but with my granddaughter I have gone back to our roots.

Question #7: How is spiritual growth related to your leadership success?
God, Creativity, and Initiative

San Juan noted that she has grown a lot spiritually. She said:

> It is in every human being's path to grow spiritually. If God give you lemons, and you'll look at the lemons

and say, "What the hell am I going to do with this?" or you can say, "Let me make some lemonade. Put a little sugar in it and ice and fresh water, and drink, body, and move on!

Question #8: Discuss your own personal motivations and influence on your ability to transform your followers.

While examining the concept of personal motivation and transforming followers, the interviewees talked about following God's path as well as placing the focus on others through modeling, learning, listening, and assisting.

Maria Sanjuan discussed the value of an ethical belief system in order to assist others to create opportunities:

> The message—I think that the message is, you know, you have to be ethical. You have to have integrity. You have to tell the truth. You know, these are big words today. . . . You see it in politics. You see it in business, and you know people aren't playing with a full deck, and you say, "Oh, my God," but then you say, "No, I cannot do it because that's not who I am," and you have to be transparent. You have to be—you have to have integrity. You have to have compassion. You have to create opportunities because you're not going to take anything with you. I promise you. Nothing.

Question #9: Did you have a mentor throughout the difficult times in your life/career? If so please discuss the benefits you received by having this mentor.

Nine of the interviewees said they had mentors throughout the difficult times in their lives or careers. In regard to this question, the interviewees discussed family and friends as well as spiritual guidance. Interviewees also explained the benefits of having mentors.

Family and Friends

Several interviewees discussed the importance of family mentors. Maria Sanjuan selected her mother as her mentor.

Question #10: Do you know other resilient, successful, transformational women who might contribute to and participate in this study? Please describe this individual or individuals.

When asked for names of other resilient, successful, transformational women leaders, the interviewees mentioned women from several areas. These areas included religion and education, politics and business, and family members and friends.

San Juan said that the one woman she would recommend who she thinks is resilient and a successful leader would have been Mayor Wasserman-Rubin, but I had already interviewed her. She also mentioned that if Margaret Thatcher or Golda Meir would be alive she would have recommended them as well.

Chapter 11

Dr. Donna Shalala

Dr. Donna Shalala was born in Cleveland, Ohio. Although she was a controversial nominee, she served as the U.S. Health and Human Services Secretary in the Clinton administration. During her tenure at HHS, she fought for more funding for AIDS research and the National Institute of Health and for welfare reform. While the Medicare trust fund issue loomed, she continued focusing on anti-tobacco and anti-drug initiatives.

Shalala also served as Chancellor of the University of Wisconsin, and during that time, the school adopted a speech code banning hate speech. She also introduced a plan to more than double the number of new minority undergraduates. A federal judge ruled the speech code unconstitutional; critics said the minority recruitment plan could lead to admission decisions based on race.

Shalala received a PhD degree from Syracuse University. She has more than thirty honorary degrees and a host of other honors, including the 1992 National Public Service Award and the *Glamour Magazine* Woman of the Year Award in 1994. She has been a Johan Simon Guggenheim Fellow and has been elected to the National Academy of Education, the National Academy of Public Administration, the American Academy of Arts and Sciences, the National Academy of Social Insurance, the Institute of Medicine, and the National Academy of Sciences.

Her previous occupations include President of Hunter College and Assistant Secretary for Policy Development and Research at the Department of Housing and Urban Development. A leading political scientist, she has held professorships at Columbia, CUNY, and the University of Wisconsin.

Question #1: Please discuss some of the adversities, difficulties, or oppositions you have experienced in your life/career.

All of the resilient, transformational, successful women leaders discussed numerous adversities, difficulties, and oppositions they experienced in their lives or careers. They described life issues and discrimination issues. They also recounted how they believed they kept focused.

Gender

Donna Shalala had a similar experience to Janet Reno's while attending graduate school and later in her professional life:

> Well, you know, like most women, I had people say to me in graduate school, "We don't want to give you any help because women don't finish their PhD," so all I did was go to the—complain to the appropriate people so the people couldn't continue to say those things like that to women. When I got my first job, the chairman of the department said, "We don't tenure women," and I just went and got myself another job.

Question #2: What kept you focused?

Work and Responsibility

Dr. Shalala also talked of her work: "So my way of getting around difficulty either is to work harder or to find another job, so I don't have to keep worrying about those people."

Question #3: How would you define resiliency?

In discussing definitions of resiliency, the interviewees talked about having the ability to bounce back or snap back, being able to accept adversity or hardship, looking to the future, and refusing to be a victim.

Dr. Shalala defined resiliency as the ability to bounce back or snap back.

Question #4: How does/how has resiliency work(ed) for you? In other words, what made you persevere and not give up?

In discussing how resiliency has worked for them, the interviewees talked about God and faith, personal determination, and meeting the expectations of others.

Donna Shalala indicated that her determination is related to being competitive. She noted: "Oh, I think that I'm just competitive. I—you know—my strategy has always been that if I hit a brick wall, to turn around and go in another direction. There's always enough to do."

Question #5: Do you have a belief regarding how resilient women survive stressors to which many succumb? Please explain.

While discussing their beliefs about how resilient women survive stressors, the interviewees mentioned life experiences, trust in God and hope, and belief in oneself and others.

Donna Shalala added, "I think resilient women have had some successes in their life, and they believe in themselves. They have strong self-images. They want to survive."

Question #6: How is personal growth related to your leadership success?

When discussing the relationship between personal growth and leadership, the interviewees focused on facilitating the work of others and learning from experiences. Dr. Shalala noted that she has learned new things from every new job.

Question #7: How is spiritual growth related to your leadership success?

Dr. Shalala related that her spiritual growth has not actually contributed much to her success. She explains:

> I mean, I have strong beliefs, but I'm not sure it had anything to do with my leadership success.

Question #8: Discuss your own personal motivations and influence on your ability to transform your followers.

While examining the concept of personal motivation and transforming followers, the interviewees talked about following God's path as well as placing the focus on others through modeling, learning, listening, and assisting.

Other interviewees remarked that there is great value in listening, learning from others and from history, as well as supporting others. For example, Donna Shalala said, "Well, I think I'm a good listener, and that I don't have to be the center of attention all the time, so that's helped a lot, and I always support people in their own growth."

Question #9: Did you have a mentor throughout the difficult times in your life/career? If so please discuss the benefits you received by having this mentor.

Nine of the interviewees said they had mentors throughout the difficult times in their lives or careers. In regard to this question, the interviewees discussed family and friends as well as spiritual guidance. Interviewees also explained the benefits of having mentors.

Dr. Shalala conveyed that she did not have a mentor or mentors throughout the difficult times in her life and her career.

Question #10: Do you know other resilient, successful, transformational women who might contribute to and participate in this study? Please describe this individual or individuals.

When asked for names of other resilient, successful, transformational women leaders, the interviewees mentioned women from several areas. These areas included religion and education, politics and business, and family members and friends.

Dr. Shalala recommended sister Jean, the president of Barry University, as a resilient, successful woman leader who might want to contribute and participate in this study.

Chapter 12

Lori St. Thomas

Lori St. Thomas serves as the principal of an inner-city pre-K through eighth-grade Catholic school in the Archdiocese of Miami. St. Thomas has dedicated several years to educating and caring for children in the South Florida area. Before assuming the responsibility of principal, she earned a bachelor's degree in nursing from Barry University in Miami Shores, Florida.

After practicing as a registered nurse, specializing in neonatal intensive care and labor and delivery, St. Thomas returned to school to earn a master's degree in elementary education. While in the master's program, she began a new, rewarding career in the field of education. She has taught at the pre-school, elementary, and middle school levels. In 1999, she began work on a PhD at Barry University, specializing in educational leadership. She will complete the PhD in 2003.

St. Thomas has been married for sixteen years and has five children ages seven to twelve. She is thirty-nine years old. Her husband is a cancer survivor who is currently undergoing treatment.

Question #1: Please discuss some of the adversities, difficulties, or oppositions you have experienced in your life/career.

All of the resilient, transformational, successful women leaders discussed numerous adversities, difficulties, and oppositions they experienced in their lives or careers. They described life issues and discrimination issues. They also recounted how they believed they kept focused.

Medical Problems

Another type of problem discussed by one interviewee was medical problems. Lori St. Thomas discussed the difficulties she faced regarding pregnancy:

> I got pregnant and had a miscarriage and then subsequently couldn't get pregnant and went on fertility drugs and got pregnant with triplets, and I lost two of them, and I kept one. At that point, the doctor said that it was not physically possible for me to have any more kids. You know, don't even think about it, and I'm blessed to have five children right now.

St. Thomas also commented about the difficulties regarding her husband's recent illness:

> My husband was diagnosed with a level two melanoma, and they told us that it looks good, that it hadn't spread, and about a month later they said that it did spread, and then he was diagnosed with thyroid cancer, and they weren't sure if the two were linked or not. Well, they did surgery, and it took about eight hours because the tumor was larger than they had anticipated once they got in there, and then they said don't worry, that more than likely it didn't spread, 97% of a chance it didn't spread, and about two weeks later, they said they were wrong and that it did spread, and he had throat cancer. Then the doctors

said that there's a possibility that the lymphatic system was involved since it had already spread to the throat, so he underwent radiation. And while he was in and out of the hospital and going through his radiation and his surgeries—he's had three surgeries and one round of radiation so far. And while he was going through all of that, I still had the five kids, and the school, and the work.

Question #2: What kept you focused?

God and Spirituality

Several interviewees pointed out that God and/or their spirituality helped to keep them focused. Lori St. Thomas remarked that she believes her faith sustains her:

> There's a really interesting expression that says, "Let go and let God." And it's a wonderful expression except it's much harder to do than to say. But when you learn to do it, and you just really learn that you are not walking your path, you're walking somebody else's. And that for me personally is how I get through. The Lord only gives me what I can handle. Sometimes I think that He knows a lot more than I know about what I can handle. . . . So, whatever I face, I face for a reason, and what that reason is I don't always know, but I don't need to know.

Education

St. Thomas mentioned that she continues to pursue her education as an example for her children:

I see education as making myself better and my life better, and I want my kids to see that that's an important
thing, that that's an important part of life that no matter
what else is going on, you have to move forward.

Question #3: How would you define resiliency?

In discussing definitions of resiliency, the interviewees talked
about having the ability to bounce back or snap back, being able
to accept adversity or hardship, looking to the future, and refusing to be a victim. St. Thomas said:

In the literal sense it is the ability to bounce back, but
I would say it is the ability to overcome any challenges
the Lord puts in front of you. And keep your eyes on the
ball; keep your feet on the path. And keep going; this is
what it means to be resilient, saying okay, you put this in
front of me for a reason, and I am going to deal with it,
and then I am going to move on. It is not so much why
did this happen to me? And I have to overcome this, and
I have to get by this . . . it is about adapting, overcoming,
making the necessary changes to stay focused.

Question #4: How does/how has resiliency work(ed) for you? In other words, what made you persevere and not give up?

In discussing how resiliency has worked for them, the interviewees talked about God and faith, personal determination, and
meeting the expectations of others.

God and Faith

Lori St. Thomas discussed her faith in the context of her family:

That is totally my faith, and very strong family.
I have a wonderful husband; he is supportive and
helpful, and my father and I have a very close relationship. You know, I have my moments, everybody
has their moments that they get down . . . for example, my husband's cancer is a very overwhelming
thing to try to deal with. . . . So, first I would say my
faith keeps me going, and my family would be my
second better factor.

Question #5: Do you have a belief regarding how resilient women survive stressors to which many succumb? Please explain.

While discussing their beliefs about how resilient women survive
stressors, the interviewees mentioned life experiences, trust in
God and hope, and belief in oneself and others.

Trust in God and Hope

Several of the interviewees discussed the idea that trust in God,
their faith, and/or a sense of hope help them to survive stressors.
As an example, Lori St. Thomas focused her answer clearly on
the thought that she keeps going because she is where God wants
her to be:

I think, and this is a personal belief, that some of the
women who succumb are very much caught up in the
I and me, and not in what the bigger picture is. I think
it would be very easy, especially for a woman in
today's society, to succumb. The questions of should
I take this job, and when you look at the comparable
level of management, you are looking at a predomi-
nantly male workforce. If you don't take it, I can see

how you can succumb. I am very blessed because
I don't care about what everybody else thinks; I care
about what I am supposed to be doing. Where I am
supposed to be now is in the Catholic school, a principal of a Catholic school; that is where the Lord has led
me right now. And that is where my focus is, and
I think that is why I don't succumb to those stressors,
because I feel that I am exactly where the Lord wants
me to be. If I worried about this person or that person,
and who has this, and who has that, then maybe my
outlook would be different. But the way I look at it is
I have enough to worry about with my husband, and
my five kids, and all my own issues, and I am happy
with what I do. And I know that what I do is what the
Lord wants me to do.

Question #6: How is personal growth related to your leadership success?

When discussing the relationship between personal growth and
leadership, the interviewees focused on facilitating the work of
others and learning from experiences.

Learning from Experiences

St. Thomas also discussed how life's experiences have influenced
her personal growth and leadership:

> I have grown personally; I have learned for one thing
> that authority helps me be effective as a leader. Would
> I have done this 20 years ago? No, I would not have
> taught in an office of maturity, and I wouldn't have had
> the patience and understanding that you need to be a
> principal. I had to go through a process; I had to have

kids of my own; and I am not saying that others that don't have kids of their own can't do it, but my personal belief is that I can empathize with the parents, the students, and the teachers and really have a true understanding of all of their issues. I taught in the classroom, and I taught pre-school, I taught in elementary, and I taught middle school. And I know what it means to have days where you just can't wait to go home. But I also know what it means to a parent to have your kid come home with six hours of homework and have that feeling like this is not right. But I would not have had that understanding unless I would have gone through this personal growth in my life. I had to take my time and be a teacher in the classroom, and I had to have mom time and know what it feels like to be pulled in 25 different directions . . . to be where I am today. And overall, I think that it has really formed me as a leader.

Question #7: How is spiritual growth related to your leadership success?
Church Beliefs

Two interviewees discussed church beliefs as part of their spiritual growth and leadership. Lori St. Thomas discussed her spiritual growth vis-à-vis her work as a Catholic school leader:

[My] personal growth is also spiritual growth. This is something that my kids will learn from me, and being a leader in a Catholic school, I want them to see that. I mean whatever religion it is, I happen to be in a Catholic school. I want the kids to understand the Catholic identity. I want them to understand the Christ-centered learning approach. And that is a major part of my life. . . . I attribute all of it to the Lord.

Question #8: Discuss your own personal motivations and influence on your ability to transform your followers.

While examining the concept of personal motivation and transforming followers, the interviewees talked about following God's path as well as placing the focus on others through modeling, learning, listening, and assisting.

Following God's Path

Lori St. Thomas discussed personal motivation:

> My personal motivation is that, I would say—and it goes back to the same response—that my personal motivation would also be walking on the path that I am walking on. That influences my abilities. I guess you would say that I want the students in this particular setting—I want them to see the bigger picture. The Lord has the whole influence because I want them to have this desire to learn about the Lord to come from within. One of two things can happen. They can either go to church and sit there and watch a Mass, or they can go to church and participate in the Mass. And they that have gotten the message and have learned that it is all in your heart and soul—the will to participate in the Mass. That is what I want for them, that is what I want for my teachers too, because if it doesn't come from within me, then I will never get it from within them. That is what I think my personal motivation is for my students, and my faculty, and it has to come from within me first.

Question #9: Did you have a mentor throughout the difficult times in your life/career? If so please discuss the benefits you received by having this mentor.

Nine of the interviewees said they had mentors throughout the difficult times in their lives or careers. In regard to this question, the interviewees discussed family and friends as well as spiritual guidance. Interviewees also explained the benefits of having mentors.

Family and Friends

Several interviewees discussed the importance of family mentors. Lori St. Thomas commented that both her father and her husband are her mentors. She stated that she learned how "to get the big picture" by watching her father.

Question #10: Do you know other resilient, successful, transformational women who might contribute to and participate in this study? Please describe this individual or individuals.

When asked for names of other resilient, successful, transformational women leaders, the interviewees mentioned women from several areas. These areas included religion and education, politics and business, and family members and friends. St. Thomas suggested Kristen Hughes, one of the participants of the current study.

Chapter 13

Rose Tydus

Rose Tydus was raised in Milwaukee, Wisconsin, and as a child, her interest was the performing arts. She spent years cultivating the art forms she loved most—ballet and jazz dance. At the age of twenty, she left Milwaukee to dance professionally. She traveled extensively, performing with noted celebrities at the nation's top hotels, resorts, and cruise lines and abroad.

In 1975, Tydus received Christ as her personal Savior and Lord and surrendered her talents to Him. At that time, liturgical dance was not accepted by her denomination, and she obediently abandoned her talent and career. Perplexed but not discouraged, she continued to serve the Lord, offering praise and worship through other art forms—poetry, singing, and production.

For the past twenty-seven years, she has ministered in song and presented the Word of God to congregations, inmates, students, and Christian television. She has also written and produced gospel programming for public television and hosted and performed on the television specials *The Gospel and All That Jazz* and *Black Folk Songs.* Tydus was the first Black City Clerk of the City of Opa-Locka, Florida. She used her talents to bring restoration and hope to a city that was experiencing highly publicized political corruption and economic and social ills. She also served full-time as CEO of the Opa-Locka Rescue Mission from 1987 until November of 2002, a ministry dedicated to evangelizing and providing food, clothing, household items, shelter, and Christian counsel to the homeless and crisis-stricken families in the city of Opa-Locka. She is presently employed as Minister of Youth and Administrator at Stanton Memorial Baptist Church in North Miami, Florida.

Tydus also serves as Vice Mayor of the city of Opa-Locka, and when she is referred to as a politician, she does not hesitate to respond by saying, "I do not consider myself a politician, but a woman who loves the Lord and wants to improve the quality of life in her community; I just happen to be Vice Mayor." Her recent accomplishments include the release of her debut CD, *Time and Seasons*, which includes innovative and impressive arrangements that are a mixture of easy listening, Latin, and jazz.

Question #1: Please discuss some of the adversities, difficulties, or oppositions you have experienced in your life/career.

All of the resilient, transformational, successful women leaders discussed numerous adversities, difficulties, and oppositions they experienced in their lives or careers. They described life issues and discrimination issues. They also recounted how they believed they kept focused.

Discrimination

Rose Tydus discussed another type of discrimination related to her status as a minority. She recounted the opposition she faced because of her religion as well as her race:

> My public service always included my Christian service, and I was appointed as the first Black city clerk of Opa-Locka. That was during a time when

racism was still very prevalent in that community, along with crime and a lot of public corruption, and I was also not really highly favored by many of my colleagues because of my Christian principles and ethics. And I experienced a tremendous amount of opposition and a lack of cooperation, even to the point of my termination after almost ten years of dedication of service . . .

Question #2: What kept you focused?

God and Spirituality

Several interviewees pointed out that God and/or their spirituality helped to keep them focused. Rose Tydus noted that she depends on God to keep her focused. After a particularly difficult situation, she explained:

I had to depend on the word of God to strengthen me and guide me to really look with expectation, great expectation that He was going to make something good out of this situation which he had promised to do in Romans 8:28 that all things work together for good for those who love the Lord and are called according to His purpose. That is what kept me focused . . .

Question #3: How would you define resiliency?

In discussing definitions of resiliency, the interviewees talked about having the ability to bounce back or snap back, being able to accept adversity or hardship, looking to the future, and refusing to be a victim.

Question #4: How does/how has resiliency work(ed) for you? In other words, what made you persevere and not give up?

In discussing how resiliency has worked for them, the interviewees talked about God and faith, personal determination, and meeting the expectations of others.

God and Faith

Rose Tydus also mentioned her faith as a factor, stating: "The word of God has just meant so very much to me, and if it wasn't for that, I would not have a basis for anything . . . the race is not won by the swift but by the one who perseveres."

Question #5: Do you have a belief regarding how resilient women survive stressors to which many succumb? Please explain.

While discussing their beliefs about how resilient women survive stressors, the interviewees mentioned life experiences, trust in God and hope, and belief in oneself and others.

Life Experiences

Rose Tydus discussed life experiences as a way of surviving stressors:

> Well, I don't think resiliency is something we are born with. It is something that is developed, and there are many different factors that determine that level or that quality of our resiliency; it has to do with our environment, our upbringing, our life experiences; even our physical and mental health has a lot to do with it.

Question #6: How is personal growth related to your leadership success?

When discussing the relationship between personal growth and leadership, the interviewees focused on facilitating the work of others and learning from experiences.

Diet

Tydus referred to the relationship of personal growth and leadership success in terms of dieting. She describes it:

> Well, I think our personal and spiritual growth is contingent upon our diet and exercise—what we put in is what we are going to be able to put out. So we need to always take advantage and put in those things that are going to improve our skills through workshops and then exercising those and putting those things into practice.

Question #7: How is spiritual growth related to your leadership success?

Tydus explains how spirituality plays a very big part of her success in leadership:

> I think that resiliency and faith have a lot in common. I remember seeing that movie, I don't know if you remember it "What's Love Got to Do with It?" about Tina Turner. Most of her life was filled with hardship and full of physical abuse inflicted by her husband and then she eventually left him, and became penniless and then a friend introduced her to Buddhism. And then she began to belief in herself and love herself and was

able to pick up the pieces, then her career began to sour again and it went beyond what it was in the beginning, but you know till this day she gives that credit to her faith and devotion to Buddha and that resiliency and transformation of her life to him. I am thinking now from a Christian perspective, we certainly have to be really careful in considering the eternal value of everything that we do in this life including how we handle adversity and difficulty in life. The objects and the author of our resiliency is going to be tested, so we have to make sure that we hear those words "well done, my good and faithful servant,' even coming out of adversity, so I think we all have the ability, because some people believe in their resiliency—that they have a strong enough constitution within themselves that they are going to or can do whatever it is.

Question #8: Discuss your own personal motivations and influence on your ability to transform your followers.

While examining the concept of personal motivation and transforming followers, the interviewees talked about following God's path as well as placing the focus on others through modeling, learning, listening, and assisting.

Following God's Path

Two interviewees talked of personal motivation and transforming followers in the context of following God's path. For instance, Rose Tydus said:

> Well, I would say for me regular church attendance and involvement. To make sure that the gifts that the Lord has

given me, that I use them in the church. . . . I enjoy listening to Christian music and radio. Those are the things that have helped to keep me where I need to be so that people will see Jesus in me and . . . God will get the glory.

Question #9: Did you have a mentor throughout the difficult times in your life/career? If so please discuss the benefits you received by having this mentor.

Nine of the interviewees said they had mentors throughout the difficult times in their lives or careers. In regard to this question, the interviewees discussed family and friends as well as spiritual guidance. Interviewees also explained the benefits of having mentors.

Spiritual Guidance

Three of the interviewees mentioned spiritual guides as mentors. Rose Tydus said Jesus is her mentor.

Benefits

Eight interviewees answered this part of the question. Anna Escobedo Cabral and Rose Tydus both mentioned that the benefits they received were that their mentors were always there for them.

Question #10: Do you know other resilient, successful, transformational women who might contribute to and participate in this study? Please describe this individual or individuals.

When asked for names of other resilient, successful, transformational women leaders, the interviewees mentioned women from

several areas. These areas included religion and education, politics and business, and family members and friends.

Religion and Education

Several of the interviewees mentioned religious leaders or leaders in education. Rose Tydus named Ella Cobbs, who is a pastor.

Chapter 14

Diana Wasserman-Rubin

Diana Wasserman-Rubin was born in Havana, Cuba, and came to the United States in 1960. She became a U.S. citizen in 1970. She is Broward County's first Hispanic woman mayor. It is not surprising because she has lived a lifetime of "firsts." She was the first Hispanic American elected to the Broward County Board of Commissioners in 2000 and the first Hispanic American to serve as Vice Chair in 2001. In 1998, she was the first Hispanic female elected countywide to the Broward County School Board. She was also the first Hispanic American to serve on the South Broward Hospital District Board of Commissioners and the first female to serve as Chair of the Board. In addition, she is the first Hispanic American to be inducted into the Women's Hall of Fame.

Wasserman-Rubin has had many recent accomplishments. She successfully chaired the 2002 Broward County Fire Rescue Council. Under her leadership, a consensus-building relationship was formed to improve and enhance the delivery of vital fire rescue services countywide. She also created the Mental Health Coalition, which is comprised of law enforcement personnel, members of the judiciary, consumers, and fund-raising activists.

Wasserman-Rubin conducts workshops and lectures. She is a motivational speaker for Aspira at the yearly Young Latinas Conference; a panelist/presenter at the Latino Summit in Atlanta, Georgia; a guest professor at Broward Community College, Florida Atlantic University, and Florida International University; and a panelist for the League of Women Voters of Broward Community College.

Question #1: Please discuss some of the adversities, difficulties, or oppositions you have experienced in your life/career.

All of the resilient, transformational, successful women leaders discussed numerous adversities, difficulties, and oppositions they experienced in their lives or careers. They described life issues and discrimination issues. They also recounted how they believed they kept focused.

Wasserman-Rubin noted that humor is a relevant part of keeping focused:

> So don't forget to smile, and don't forget to laugh, and don't forget to smell the roses.

Minority Problems

Several interviewees discussed discrimination related to their status as minorities. For example, Diana Wasserman-Rubin talked of not being accepted because of language problems:

> When I came here from Cuba at the age of 14, I was fluent in three languages; none of them was English, however. I was fluent in Spanish, French, and Latin because I went to a Catholic school in my country, so I went—I wound up in Miami Beach at Nautilus Junior High School—and at that time, there were no bilingual programs. There were no transitional programs to assist the very many kids that were coming in from Cuba through the Peter Pan process or with their parents. . . . If you can remember when you were 14 years old how

important it was that you had your friends and your social life. You were beginning to form your social connections and relationships. I left all of that behind, and I came to a country where there was not a lot of acceptance for me or any other people that perhaps did not converse in the native language, so it became—my social life was nonexistent. My grades began to suffer, and I was an honor roll student in Havana in Cuba, and so I felt pretty little, pretty small, pretty inconsequential, and I lost all my self-esteem . . .

Question #2: What kept you focused?
Sense of Humor

Diana Wasserman-Rubin also talked of the value of humor:

By the way, if you do not have a sense of humor, I used to tell my friends all the time, "The minute I don't laugh at a joke or I don't tell a joke, take me out back and shoot me," because levity can get you by. I have gotten out of some really serious corners with a little bit of levity. So don't forget to smile, and don't forget to laugh, and don't forget to smell the roses.

Question #3: How would you define resiliency?

In discussing definitions of resiliency, the interviewees talked about having the ability to bounce back or snap back, being able to accept adversity or hardship, looking to the future, and refusing to be a victim.

Diana Wasserman-Rubin defined resiliency as the ability to bounce back or snap back. She added that besides just bouncing back, people with resiliency "bounce back stronger than you were before the situation occurred."

Question #4: How does/how has resiliency work(ed) for you? In other words, what made you persevere and not give up?

In discussing how resiliency has worked for them, the interviewees talked about God and faith, personal determination, and meeting the expectations of others.

Diana Wasserman-Rubin discussed her belief that determination is related to self-esteem, saying: "People give up easily because they don't have a sufficient amount of self-esteem. Self-esteem is something that's really difficult to learn, but I think self-esteem is more taught than anything else. . ."

Question #5: Do you have a belief regarding how resilient women survive stressors to which many succumb? Please explain.

While discussing their beliefs about how resilient women survive stressors, the interviewees mentioned life experiences, trust in God and hope, and belief in oneself and others.

Diana Wasserman-Rubin noted that she is not in control of everything and this is a good concept to understand. She discussed what she calls the "three C's":

> I didn't cause it, I can't cure it, and I can't control it. That has guided me through years of difficult times so that I can still face the music every morning, do my job, and advocate for the community. I didn't cause it, I can't cure it, and I can't control it. Once you identify those three, say it to yourself in your head, you say, "Okay." Then next, because you're not going to spend your good, positive energy on trying to fix something that has no cure, that you can't feel guilty about because you didn't cause it, and you can't control it. You get on.

Question #6: How is personal growth related to your leadership success?

When discussing the relationship between personal growth and leadership, the interviewees focused on facilitating the work of others and learning from experiences.

Facilitating the Work of Others

Diana Wasserman-Rubin indicated that personal growth has led to the respect she has earned as a leader:

> I think the more respect that I get from the community as I do my job—and I have been getting a lot of accolades on my leadership style. I am a conciliatory person. I am a census builder. I try to bring people together. I speak at the end. I don't usurp anybody's opportunity to speak, and I gained over the last 20-some-odd years the respect of the community.

Question #7: How is spiritual growth related to your leadership success?
Spirituality as it Relates to the Self

Wasserman-Rubin discussed how she had been raised as a Catholic but believes in other kinds of spirituality—that which comes from the self as well as spirituality as an expression of art:

> That's the only religion [Catholicism] I practiced in my life, but I don't believe that religion—organized religion in and of itself—is the only provider of spiritualism. . . . Spiritualism comes from within. Whatever appeals to you, if it's Buddhism, Hinduism, Catholicism, Judaism, any religion, it's fine. . . . You express your spiritualism through your art, if you sing, you dance, you move your

hands, you express by words, you write books, you
know, you're a creative writer, a painter. . . . I'm like, you
know, I do all that stuff, and I feel better, and it also gives
me strength. Spiritualism gives me a lot of strength, and
I do read a lot of . . . spiritual thoughts for the day, you
know, those kinds of things. Sometimes they don't click
with me, but other times I read something, and it takes
me through the whole day.

Wasserman-Rubin also talked of listening and learning:

I think I'm good at persuading people. I've learned,
like I said at the beginning, from others what is—what
has been effective for other leaders—and I've taken
ideas from other great people, and great people
throughout history that I've admired and I've listened
to. Some have been men. Some have been women.

She added, "If they respect me, they will listen to me. If they
listen to me, I have a chance to persuade them. If they don't
respect, I don't get to first base."

Question #8: Discuss your own personal motivations and influence on your ability to transform your followers.

While examining the concept of personal motivation and transforming followers, the interviewees talked about following God's
path as well as placing the focus on others through modeling,
learning, listening, and assisting.

Listening, Respect and Persuasion

Wasserman-Rubin describes her own personal motivation and
influences on her ability to lead and transform her followers:

I think I'm good at persuading people. I've learned, like I said at the beginning, from others what is—what has been effective for other leaders, and I've taken ideas from other great people throughout history that I've admired and I've listened to. Some have been men. Some have been women.

Wasserman-Rubin added:

I have an interesting story, I went to Tallahassee to fight for the ERA, for women's rights, I called my mom and I said, "Mom, I'm going to Tallahassee with the ERA, and I just wanted to tell you." She said, "Yes. What's the problem?" I said, "Well, there's no problem. I just wanted to tell you in case you see my face on TV you know that I'm there to support women's right to choose," and I swallowed hard and I said, "Oh, my God. What is the going to think?" Because, my mother and I never talked about things that had to do with sex, you just don't talk about that in our culture to our children. That's one of the things I changed when I was raising my children. I think it's perfectly natural to talk to your children about these things so schools don't have to take the responsibility and do it. It should be done at home based on your values and your morals at an age-appropriate level.

So I told her, and I just held my breath, and when I said, "I'm going to fight for women's reproductive rights," she said, "Good for you." That was the only time—the first time I have heard my mother react or knew her position on the issue, and I called her out of respect because even though I personally would not choose abortion, I don't believe that I have the right to tell another woman based on whatever that circumstance is or judge anybody else, and I think it should

be between that woman and her God, that women and
her family, her husband, whatever. You transform your
follower by respect, whether you believe that value or
not. If you respect me, you will listen to me. If you listen to me, I have a chance to persuade you. If they
don't respect, I don't get to first base.

Question #9: Did you have a mentor throughout the difficult times in your life/career? If so please discuss the benefits you received by having this mentor.

Nine of the interviewees said they had mentors throughout the
difficult times in their lives or careers. In regard to this question,
the interviewees discussed family and friends as well as spiritual
guidance. Interviewees also explained the benefits of having
mentors.

Family and Friends

Several interviewees discussed the importance of family mentors.
Diana Wasserman-Rubin said that many people have helped
her throughout her life and career by believing in her. She stated
that the greatest benefit for her was that her mentors believed
in her.

Question #10: Do you know other resilient, successful, transformational women who might contribute to and participate in this study/? Please describe this individual or individuals.

When asked for names of other resilient, successful, transformational women leaders, the interviewees mentioned women from

several areas. These areas included religion and education, politics and business, and family members and friends.

Politics and Business

Diana Wasserman-Rubin named Maria Sanjuan, also one of the participants of the current study.

Chapter 15

Summary of Findings

Organized by the interview questions and the resulting sub-themes, a summary of the findings from this study follows:

Question #1: Please discuss some of the adversities, difficulties, or oppositions you have experienced in your life/career.

Question #2: What kept you focused?

All of the resilient, transformational, successful women leaders discussed numerous adversities, difficulties, and oppositions they experienced in their lives or careers. They described life issues and discrimination issues. They also recounted how they believed they kept focused. When the interviewees discussed how they believed they kept focused, they mentioned God and spirituality, family, education, work and responsibility, purpose, and sense of humor.

Question #3: How would you define resiliency?

In discussing definitions of resiliency, the interviewees talked about having the ability to bounce back or snap back, being able to accept adversity or hardship, looking to the future, and refusing to be a victim.

Question #4: How does/how has resiliency work(ed) for you? In other words, what made you persevere and not give up?

In discussing how resiliency has worked for them, the interviewees talked about God and faith, personal determination, and meeting the expectations of others.

Question #5: Do you have a belief regarding how resilient women survive stressors to which many succumb? Please explain.

While discussing their beliefs about how resilient women survive stressors, the interviewees mentioned life experiences, trust in God, hope, and belief in oneself and others and breaking traditions.

Question #6: How is personal growth related to your leadership success?

When discussing the relationship between personal growth and leadership, the interviewees focused on facilitating the work of others and learning from experiences and maintaining a healthful diet.

Question #7: How is spiritual growth related to your leadership success?

When the interviewees pondered spiritual growth and leadership, they mentioned church beliefs; God, divine guidance, and prayer; creativity and initiative; and spirituality as it relates to the self.

Question #8: Discuss your own personal motivations and influence on your ability to transform your followers.

While examining the concept of personal motivation and transforming followers, the interviewees talked about following God's path as well as placing the focus on others through modeling, learning, listening, respect and persuasion, and assisting.

Question #9: Did you have a mentor throughout the difficult times in your life/career? If so please discuss the benefits you received by having this mentor.

Nine of the interviewees said they had mentors throughout the difficult times in their lives or careers. In regard to this question, the interviewees discussed family and friends as well as spiritual guidance. Interviewees also explained the benefits of having mentors.

Question #10: Do you know other resilient, successful, transformational women who might contribute to and participate in this study? Please describe this individual or individuals.

When asked for names of other resilient, successful, transformational women leaders, the interviewees mentioned women from several areas. These areas included religion, education, politics, business, as well as family members and friends.

Discussion
Adversities and Keeping Focused

The interviewees discussed numerous adversities, difficulties, and oppositions they experienced in their lives and careers, describing life issues and discrimination issues. Several interviewees experienced discrimination because of gender. This finding is similar to Powell's (1998) study, which indicated that gender biases and the "old boys' networks" are problems women continue to face. Interviewees noted that they kept focused through God and spirituality, family, education, work and responsibility, a sense of purpose, and a sense of humor. They also maintained educational and professional support systems. The findings of the current study show that the interviewees were action oriented, gathered required resources, and acquired an education to achieve their positions. The concept of purpose and responsibility is consistent with Coutu's (2002) belief that resilient people have "strongly held values, [and believe] that life is meaningful" (p. 48). Several interviewees discussed their work as a way of focusing. Similarly, Maddux (1995) noted that individuals with high self-efficacy (resiliency) concentrate on their work rather than themselves. Interviewees also explained the importance of family in keeping focused and remaining resilient. McCubbin et al. (1998) likewise related family relationships to resiliency.

Defining Resiliency

The interviewees defined resiliency as the ability to bounce or snap back, to accept adversity, to look to the future, and not be a victim. The interviewees' perceptions of resiliency are supported by a large body of previous research in the area of resiliency, particularly the model observed in the study by Coutu (2002), which states that almost all theories overlap in three ways. This resiliency model indicated that resilient people possess three characteristics: a staunch acceptance of reality, having purpose, and having an ability to improvise. The author emphasized that one can bounce back from hardship with just one or two of these qualities, but one will only be truly resilient with all three.

The interviewees' definitions of resiliency and their beliefs about attributes and qualities of resiliency validate the importance of the concepts advocated in the resiliency models. Furthermore, the findings help to provide answers to questions such as those posed by Coutu (2002). How do people who face difficulty, adversity, or opposition experience resiliency and become successful? What exactly is that quality of resilience that carries them through life? And how does resiliency work?

The findings of the current study are relevant because the perceptions are from the vantage point of identified resilient, transformational, successful women leaders. The interviewees' beliefs add to the body of knowledge about resiliency attributes. The questions posed by Coutu (2002)—what exactly is that quality of resilience that carries people through life, and how does resiliency work—have been clarified by the interviewees in their responses, such as "the reality of taking one day at a time," "living a life of purpose for God," and resilience through "competitiveness."

Furthermore, the findings of the current study indicate that the interviewees perceived that certain behaviors and/or qualities constitute a resilient person, including: having the drive to succeed; wanting to surface again and not give up; maintaining an innate competitiveness; and continuing the perseverance that was instilled by their families.

Congruent with the interviewees' definitions, the resiliency models indicated that resilient survivors avoid adverse outcomes through ego resilience (resourceful, flexible responses to novel or stressful situations as measured by the California Q-set) (Block, 1991). Additionally, consistent with the findings of the current study, Werner (1984) defined resiliency as "the ability to recover from or adjust easily to misfortune or sustained life stress" (p. 68). Masten et al. (1990) defined resiliency as "a process, capacity, or outcome of successful adaptation despite challenges or threatening circumstances . . . good outcome despite high risk status, sustained competence under threat and recovery from trauma" (p. 426).

It is interesting to note that the definitions of resiliency and the qualities attributed to resilience provided by the interviewees indicated that it is important to accept adversity as part of life, to step through it and beyond it with courage. They noted that determination and trust were important factors in not becoming a victim. The concept of accepting adversity as a part of life is consistent with Coutu's (2002) "acceptance of reality" (p. 48) and Maddux's (1995) belief that resilient individuals approach difficulties as challenges to be mastered rather than threats to be avoided.

Persevering and Surviving Stressors

In their discussions of perseverance and surviving stressors, the interviewees mentioned God and spirituality, determination, belief in the self and others, and meeting the expectations of others. The finding linking resilience with spirituality is consistent with findings from Ramsey and Blieszner's (1999) study indicating that the women they interviewed exhibited resiliency because of their ability to intertwine thinking and feelings about the past, present, and future and their ability to relate personally to people and God.

These findings additionally expand on previous research (Block, 1991; Garmezy, 1993; Werner & Smith, 1992) that found that resilient survival of excessive stress is attributed to personal characteristics such as coping strategies, intelligence, physiological reactivity, and temperament. The findings of the current study are also supported by Walker's (1993) study, which investigated the meaning of personal success for a group of women who came to middle age in the second half of the twentieth century. The study participants provided insight into the meaning of success and achievement for those who value personal time, family life, career advancement, and community involvement. Several themes that emerged in Walker's study include valuing connection and continuity in relationships, balancing care and responsibility, and working to make a difference.

Personal and Spiritual Growth

Regarding personal and spiritual growth, the interviewees discussed learning to grow from experience, helping others, and having a personal spirituality. Findings of the current study indicated that most interviewees believe that personal growth is very important to leadership success, and a key characteristic for that success is ability to change. One interviewee stated, "By human nature we are resistant to change, but as difficult as it is for a leader, you are the one that has to change." Regarding the importance of being flexible in order to change, Rutter (1993) explored various conceptual considerations of resiliency. He described resiliency as a changing characteristic, noting that it results from repeated incidents of successful coping with stressors such as change, not from avoidance of stressors.

Several interviewees of the current study indicated that they have learned much from personal experience. This is consistent with the thinking of Bandura (1995). As noted, self-efficacy is often used interchangeably with resiliency (Bandura, 1995; Maddux, 1995; Schwarzer, 1992). According to Bandura, there are four ways of developing a strong sense of efficacy; the most effective is through mastery of experiences. Successes build a belief in one's efficacy, and failures undermine it. Therefore, if one experiences only easy successes, one will be easily discouraged by failure.

Another finding of the current study indicated that the influence of God, faith, religion, and/or church was relevant for nine of the interviewees. One interviewee commented that she had to depend on the Word of God to strengthen and guide her. Another stated, "Without spiritual growth, I would not be anywhere. Without God, I would not be able to do anything; He is my father, and the captain in my life." It is interesting to note that the perceptions of the interviewees of the current study regarding spirituality and leadership are valuable because their viewpoints are consistent with previous research in the area of leadership, particularly transformational leadership (Bass, 1990; Burns, 1978), servant leadership (Greenleaf, 1977), and spiritual leadership (Bolman & Deal, 1995). These leadership models advocate similar concepts such as service; having consistent values and behaviors; having concern for the least privileged of society;

leading others to greater morality; believing in concepts such as caring for the soul, dialogue, and listening; and leading for community building.

The interviewees' beliefs about spiritual growth validate the importance of the concepts advocated in the above-mentioned leadership models. Furthermore, the findings help to provide answers to questions such as those posed by Fox (1994), Hawley (1993), and Senge (1990): How are personal and spiritual growth components of leadership development?

Additionally, the findings of the current study are supported by Ramsey and Blieszner's (1999) model of spiritual resiliency in women through the lifespan. In the Ramsey and Bleiszner study, participants indicated that they developed strength to bounce back from life's adversities, oppositions, or difficulties by exhibiting resilience and strong spiritual faith "in spite of" and/or "because of" the challenges, struggles, and problems they encountered. These problems included the death of children, parents, siblings, and spouses; deteriorating health, including mental health problems; loneliness; fear; and living in poverty. This study indicated that women participants were resilient because of their ability to relate personally to God, because of knowing the purpose of their lives, and because they knew that hope exists because of their faith in God, a faith that goes beyond the present life into eternity.

Leadership and Transforming Followers

Regarding leadership and the transformation of followers, interviewees emphasized following God's path and placing the focus on others through modeling, learning, listening, and assisting. Interviewees of the current study pointed out that in order for leaders to be effective in the twenty-first century, they will need to embrace values consistent with service and a demonstrated ethic of care toward others, to recognize the interdependence among all people, and to foster personal empowerment.

The concept of focusing on others and caring is similar to Forbes' (1993) Theory F Transformational Leadership Model, which gives credit to a woman's style of leading. It identifies the need for the managerial and political aspects of leadership while simultaneously encouraging women to lead with care and compassion. Bass and Aviolo (1994) contended that transformational leaders align their own personal principles with those of the group, organization, and society. This notion suggests that transformational leaders operate from a value-driven personal philosophy and advocate concepts such as service to followers and others; empowering others to grow; being change agents; and taking risks.

Mentors

Nine of the interviewees said they had mentors throughout the difficult times in their lives or careers. Interviewees discussed family and friends as well as spiritual guidance. Five interviewees mentioned the importance of family mentors; four selected their mothers. This might be explained because children have traditionally spent more time with their mothers, and mothers are often regarded as the moral and spiritual guides of families. One interviewee described her mother as "a woman with tremendous determination." Another stated, "My mother gave me strength that she will never understand." Reliance on family for support is similar to McCubbin, McCubbin, and Thompson's (1992) discussion of the processes that promote family endurance, coping, and survival. Garmezy (1993) noted that protection factors are found not only in the person but in the family and community as well.

Eight interviewees discussed the benefits of having mentors. Two interviewees explained that the benefits were that their mentors were always there for them. Another mentioned that mentors gave her good guidance, great wisdom, and strong support. An interviewee said that she learned how to get the big picture by watching her father, and another professed that the spirit guides her. Realizing the benefits of having a mentor is consistent with Koenig's (1997) study, which found that two-thirds of the study group (leaders with mentors) felt that their mentors made important contributions to their career successes.

Chapter 16

Conclusions

A number of conclusions can be drawn from the findings of this book:

1. Blechman, Prinz, and Dumas (1995) asserted that coping, competence, and aggression prevention, the resiliency phenomenon, so defined, applies across the lifespan to survivors of acute and chronic stressors and risk factors. Therefore, the interviewees of the current book may well serve as examples of resilient leaders.

2. The interviewees' definitions of resiliency and their beliefs about attributes and qualities of resilient, transformational, successful women validate the importance of the concepts advocated in the discussed resiliency and leadership models.

3. The findings help to provide answers to such questions as those posed by Coutu (2002): What exactly is that quality of resilience that carries people through life, and how does resiliency work?

4. Resilient women survive stressors to which many succumb by creating a new reality that will get them through the next few minutes, hours, or days; by being goal oriented; by having the drive to succeed; by not being victims or asking why did this happen to me; and by not making excuses.

5. Positive effects of personal growth result from repeated incidents of successful coping with stressors such as change, not from avoidance of stressors.

6. Personal motivations influence one's ability to transform one's followers. While examining the concept of personal motivation and transforming followers, the interviewees talked about following God's path as well as placing the focus on others through modeling, learning, listening, and assisting.

7. Spirituality is an important component of resiliency.

8. Leadership programs need to teach women the importance of mentoring and how to mentor.

9. Early role models and one's family, as well as non-family factors, help shape the self-confidence of the potential leader. Events that are unique to individual development interacting with events common to an entire population can affect the type of leader a person will become.

10. The findings build on Garmezy's (1993) concept that during life-changing turning points, resilient survivors' protection levels increase due to a caring mentor, a supportive spouse, or a religious conversion.

Appendix A

Theory F Transformational Leadership Model

Leads From a Foundation of Transformative Values and Principles

1. Committed to values such as the ethic of care and justice, equality, human dignity, diversity, interdependence, empowerment, ecology and peace; is against oppression of any kind
2. Dedicated to service for the common good
3. Understands and supports the interconnectedness of individuals, organizations, society, and the planet
4. Lives with integrity and authenticity
5. Determined to reconstruct knowledge and systems to include a feminine perspective and to work in equal and respectful partnership with men
6. Strives to live a balanced life; attends to body, mind, emotion, and spirit; integrates both feminine and masculine characteristics; balances personal and professional lives
7. Defines success in her/his own terms and according to transformative values

Demonstrates Fundamental Management and Leadership Characteristics

- has deep sense of self; is self-aware
- is confident, yet humble and constantly learning
- possesses time, organizational, and communication skills
- has high standards and models them; is responsible
- is a person of vision, courage, and conviction; inspires others to act
- listens, empathizes, and trusts; builds a sense of community and collaboration
- is skilled in decision making, group and political processes
- relies on personal rather than positional power
- emphasizes both tasks and relationships, people and productivity
- is a risk taker and change agent; gets results
- can handle conflict, ambiguity, complexity, and paradox
- incorporates play, celebrations, humor, metaphors, and symbols into her/his leadership style
- honors intuition, imagination, feelings, and other ways of knowing
- varies his/her style depending on the situation but remains true to her/his values

Githens, S. (1996).

Appendix B

Origin of Theory F Transformational Leadership Model

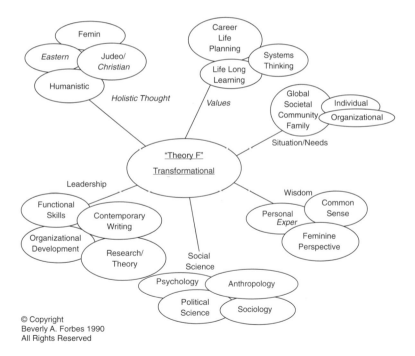

References

Anderson, C.R. (1984). *Management: Skills, functions, and organization performance.* Dubuque, IA: Wm. D. Brown Publishers.

Asmussen, K.J., & Cresswell, J.W. (1995). Campus response to a student gunman. *Journal of Higher Education, 66,* 575–591.

Avolio, B.J., Waldman, D.A., & Yammarino, F.J. (1991). Leading in the 1990s: The four I's of transformational leadership. *Journal of European Industrial Training,* 15(4), 9–16.

Bandura, A. (ed.). (1995). *Self-efficacy in changing societies.* New York: Cambridge University Press.

Bandura, A. (1997). *Self-efficacy: The exercise of control.* New York: Freeman.

Bass, B.M. (1985). *Leadership and performance beyond expectations.* New York: Free Press.

Bass, B.M. (1990). *Bass and Stogdill's handbook of leadership: Theory, research, and managerial applications* (3rd ed.). New York: Free Press.

Bass, B.M., & Avolio, B.J. (1994). *Improving organizational effectiveness through transformational leadership.* Thousand Oaks, CA: Sage.

Beardslee, W.R. (1989). The role of self-understanding in resilient individuals: The development of a perspective. *American Journal of Orthopsychiatry, 59*(2), 266–278.

Bennis, W.G. (1994). Where have all the leaders gone? In W.E. Rosenback & R.L. Taylor (eds.), *Contemporary issues in leadership,* pp. 40–52. Boulder, CO: Westview Press.

Bennis, W. (1998). *On becoming a leader*. London: Arrow.

Berg, B.L. (1995). *Qualitative research methods for the social sciences*. Boston: Allyn and Bacon.

Blake, R.R., & Mouton, J.S. (1964). *The managerial grid*. Houston, TX: Gulf.

Blake, R.R., & Mouton, J.S. (1978). *The new managerial grid*. Houston, TX: Gulf.

Blanchard, K.H., Gates, P., & Hersey, P. (1976). Diagnosing educational leadership problems: A situational approach. *Educational leadership*, (2), 348–354.

Blanchard, K.H., & Hersey, P. (1970). A leadership theory for educational administrators. *Education*, (4), 303–310.

Blanchard, K.H., & Hersey, P. (1973). The importance of communication patterns in implementing change strategies. *Journal of Research and Development in Education*, (4), 66–75.

Blechman, E.A., Prinz, R.J., & Dumas, J.E. (1995). Coping, competence, and aggression prevention: I. Developmental model. *Applied and Preventive Psychology, 4,* 211–232.

Block, J. (1991, December). *Remarks on resilience and ego resilience*. Paper presented at National Institute of Mental Health Conference on Fostering Resilience, Washington, D.C.

Blocker, S.I., & Copeland, E.P. (1994). Determinants of resilience in high-stressed youth. *High School Journal*, 77(4), April–May 286–293.

Bolig, R., & Weddle, K. (1988). Resiliency and hospitalization of children. *Children's Health Care, 16*(4), 255–260.

Bolman, L.G., & Deal, T.E. (1992). Reframing leadership: The effects of leaders' images of leadership. In K.E. Clark, M.B. Clark, & D.P. Campbell (eds.), *Impact of leadership*, pp. 72–85. Greensboro, NC: Center for Creative Leadership.

Bolman, L.G., & Deal, T.E. (1995). *Leading with soul: An uncommon journey of spirit.* (1st ed.) New York: Wiley.

Braun, B. (2000). [Book review on spiritual resiliency]. *Family Relations, 49*(3), p. 353.

Brisken, A. (1996). *The stirring of the soul in the workplace.* San Francisco: Jossey-Bass.

Brooks, J.S., Brook, D.W., Win, P.T., Whiteman, M., Masci, J.R., DeCatalogne, J., Roberto, J., & Amundsen, F. (1995). Coping with AIDS: A longitudinal study. *American Journal on Addictions, 6,* 11–20.

Brooks-Gunn, J. (1988). Antecedents and consequences of variations in girls' maturational timing. *Journal of Adolescent Health Care, 9,* 365–373.

Brooks-Gunn, J., & Chase-Lansdale, P.L. (1991). Children having children: Effects on the family system. *Pediatric Annals, 20*(9), 467–481.

Brown, E.R. (1991). Community action for health promotion: A strategy to empower individuals and communities. *International Journal of Health Services, 21*(3), 441–455.

Brown, R.T., Poepke, K.J., & Kaslow, N.J. (1993). Risk resistance-adaptation model for pediatric chronic illness: Sickle cell syndrome as an example. *Clinical Psychology Review 13,* 119–132.

Burns, J.M. (1978). *Leadership.* New York: Harper & Row.

Chemers, M.M. (1997). *An integrative theory of leadership.* Mahwah, NJ: Lawrence Erlbaum.

Ciulla, J.B. (1995). Leadership ethics: Mapping the territory. *Business Ethics Quarterly, 5*(1), 5–28.

Compas, B.E., Hiden, B.R., & Gerhardt, C.A. (1995). Adolescent development: Pathways and processes of risk and resilience. *Annual Review of Psychology, 46,* 265–293.

Conduct Problems Prevention Research Group. (1992). A developmental and clinical model for the prevention of conduct disorder: The FAST track program. *Development and Psychopathology, 4,* 509–527.

Cormier, C. (1997). *The resilience of patriarchy: Middle class membership as a necessary condition in the political success of women.* New Brunswick, Canada: University of New Brunswick.

Cortazzi, M. (1993). *Narrative analysis.* London: The Falmer Press.

Coutu, D.L. (2002, May). HBR at large: How resilience works. *Harvard Business Review, 80*(5), 46–49.

Covey, S.R. (2004). *The seven habits of highly effective people.* New York: Simon & Schuster.

Covey, S.R. (1990). *Principle-centered leadership.* New York: Simon & Schuster.

Cowen, E.L. (1991). In pursuit of wellness. *American Psychologist, 46*(4), 404–408.

Cowen, E.L., & Work, W.C. (1988). Resilient children, psychological wellness, and primary prevention. *American Journal of Community Psychology, 16*(4), 591–607.

Creswell, J.W. (2002). *Educational research.* Upper Saddle River, NJ: Merrill/Prentice Hall.

Curtis, C. (2002). Leadership is an emotional craft. *Community College Week, 14*(15), p. 5.

Dansereau, F. (1995). Leadership: The multiple-level approaches (Parts I and II). *Leadership Quarterly, 6,* 97–450.

Day, D.V., & Lord, R.G. (1988). Executive leadership and organizational performance: Suggestions for a new theory and methodology. *Journal of Management, 14,* 111–122.

Denzin, N.K., & Lincoln, Y.S. (1998). *Handbook of qualitative research.* Thousand Oaks, CA: Sage.

Dukerich, J.M., Nichols, M.L., Elm, D.R., & Vollrath, D.A. (1990). Moral reasoning in groups: Leaders make a difference. *Human Relations, 43*(5), 473–493.

Dusenbury, L., & Botvin, G.J. (1992). Substance abuse prevention: Competence enhancement and the development of positive life options. *Journal of Addictive Diseases, 11*(3), 29–45.

Eagly, A.H., & Johnson, B.T. (1990). Gender and leadership style: A meta-analysis. *Psychological Bulletin, 108,* 233–256.

Eagly, A.H., Makhijani, M.G., & Klonsky, B.G. (1992). Gender and the evaluation of leaders: A meta-analysis. *Psychological Bulletin, 3,* 3–22.

Egeland, B., Carlson, E., Collins, W.A., & Sroufe, L.A. (2005). *The Development of the Person: The Minnesota Study of Risk and Adaptation from Birth to Adulthood.* New York: Guilford Publications.

Elder, G.H., Jr. (1985). Perspectives on the life course. In G.H. Elder, Jr. (ed.), *Life course dynamics: Trajectories and transitions, 1968–1980,* pp. 23–44. Ithaca, NY: Cornell University Press.

Errante, A. (2002). But sometime you're not part of the story: Oral histories and ways of remembering and telling. *Educational Researcher, 29,* 16–27.

Fiedler, F.E. (1964). A contingency model of leadership effectiveness. In L. Berkowitz (ed.), *Advances in experimental social psychology*, vol. I, pp. 149–190. New York: Academic Press.

Fiedler, F.E. (1967). *A theory of leadership effectiveness.* New York: McGraw-Hill.

Fiedler, F.E. (1997). Situational control and a dynamic theory of leadership. In K. Grint (ed.), *Leadership: Classical, contemporary and critical approaches*. Oxford: Oxford University Press.

Fiedler, F.E., & Garcia, J.E. (1987). *New approaches to effective leadership: Cognitive resources and organizational performance.* New York: John Wiley.

Fincham, S. (1992). Community health promotion programs. *Social Science in Medicine, 35*(3), 239–249.

Fine, S.B. (1991). Resilience and human adaptability: Who rises above adversity? *The American Journal of Occupational Therapy, 45*(6), 493–503.

Fonagy, P., Steele, H., Steele, M., Higgitt, A., Target, M. (1994). *The theory and practice of psychoanalysis.* Thousand Oaks, CA: Sage Publications.

Forbes, B. (1993). *Profile of the leader of the future: Origin, premises, values and characteristics of the Theory F Transformational Leadership Model.*Unpublished manuscript.

Fortin, J., Groleau, G., O'Neill, M., Lemieux, V., Cardinal, L., & Racine, P. (1992, Fall). Quebec's healthy communities projects: The ingredients of success. *Health Promotion,* (1), 6–11.

Fox, M. (1994). *The reinvention of work: A new vision of livelihood for our time.* New York: HarperCollins.

Gardner, J. (1989) *On leadership.* New York: Free Press.

Garmezy, N. (1991a). Resilience in children's adaptation to negative life events and stressed environments. *Pediatric Annals, 20*(9), 462–466.

Garmezy, N. (1991b). Resiliency and vulnerability to adverse developmental outcomes associated with poverty. *American Behavioral Scientist, 34,* 416–430.

Garmezy, N. (1993). Children in poverty: Resilience despite risk. *Psychiatry, 56,* 12–136.

Garraty, J.A., & Sterstein, J. (1974). *Encyclopedia of American Biography.* New York: Harper & Row.

Gerth, H.H., & Mills, C. Wright (eds.). (1991). *From Max Weber. Essays in sociology.* London: Routledge.

Githens, S. (1996). *Listening to women's voices: Exploring the connection between leadership, personal growth and mountaineering.* Seattle, WA: Seattle University.

GLOBE. (1999). Impact of societal and organizational processes on leadership: The Globe study. In W. Mobley, M.J. Gessman, & V. Arnold (eds.), *Advances in global leadership*, vol. 1, pp. 171–233. Stamford, CT: JAI Press.

Greenleaf, R.K. (1977). *Servant leadership: A journey into legitimate power and greatness.* New York: Paulist Press.

Greenleaf, R.K. (1996). In D.M. Frinck & L.C. Spears (eds.). The private writings of Robert K. Greenleaf: *on becoming a servant leader.* San Francisco: Jossey-Bass.

Guba, E.G., & Lincoln, Y.S. (1989). *Fourth generation evaluation.* Newbury Park, CA: Sage Publications.

Hawley, J. (1993). *Reawakening the spirit in work.* New York: Fireside, Simon & Schuster.

Heifetz, R.A. (1994). *Leadership without easy answers.* Cambridge, MA: Belknap Press.

Hemphill, J.K. (1949). *Situational factors in leadership.* Columbus, OH: Bureau of Educational Research. Monograph 32.

Hemphill, J., & Coons, A.E. (1957). In R.M. Stogdill & E. Coons (eds.), *Leader behavior: Its description and measurement*, pp. 6–38. Columbus, OH: Bureau of Business Research Ohio State University pp. 6–38.

Herrenkohl, E.C., Herrenkohl, R.C., & Egolf, B. (1994). Resilient early school-age children from maltreating homes: Outcome in late adolescence. *American Journal of Orthopsychiatry, 64*, 301–309.

Hersey, P. (1976). Situational leadership: Some aspects of its influence on organizational development. *Dissertation Abstracts International*, (1), 438a.

Hersey, P. (1984). *The situational leader.* New York: Warner.

Hersey, P., & Blanchard, K.H. (1988). *Management of organizational behavior: Utilizing human resources* (5th ed.). New Jersey: Prentice Hall.

Hollander, E.P., & Offermann, L.R. (1990). Power and leadership in organizations: Relationships in transition. *American Psychologist, 45,* 179–189.

House, R.J., Hanges, P.J., Ruiz-Quintanallia, A., Dorfman, P., Javidan, J., Josselson, R., & Lieblich, A. (eds.). (1993). *The narrative study of lives* (vol. 1). Thousand Oaks, CA: Sage Publications.

Kandel, E., Mednick, S.A., Kirkegaard-Sorensen, L., Hutchings, B., Knop, J., Resenberg, R., & Schulsinger, F. (1998). IQ as a protective factor for subjects as high risk for antisocial behavior. *Journal of Consulting and Clinical Psychology 56,* 224–226.

King, P.M. (1997). Character and civic education: What does it take? *Educational Record, 78*(3–4), 87–93.

Kirkham, G. (1999). *Reports on books. School leadership & management* (vol. 19), p. 515.

Klein, K.J., & House, R.J. (1995). On fire: Charismatic leadership and levels of analysis. *Leadership Quarterly, 6,* 183–198.

Koenig, L.A. (1997). Perceptions of success and mentoring relationships among a selected group of women leaders in Texas. Doctoral dissertation, Texas A&M University–Kingsville. *Dissertation Abstracts International, 35*(4), 932.

Kolenko, T.A., Porter, G., Wheatley, W., & Colby, M. (1996). A critique of service learning projects in management education: Pedagogical foundations, barriers, and guidelines. *Journal of Business Ethics, 15*(1), 133–142.

Kouzes, J., & Posner, B. (1995). *The leadership challenge: How to get extraordinary things done in organizations.* San Francisco: Jossey-Bass.

Krefting, L. (1999). Rigor in qualitative research: The assessment of trustworthiness. In A.K. Milinki (ed.), *Cases in qualitative research: Research reports for discussion and evaluation.* Los Angeles: Pyrczak Publishing.

Krovetz, M.L. (1999). *Fostering resiliency.* Thousand Oaks, CA: Corwin Press.

Lawson, E.J. (1999). Resiliency in African American families. *Journal of Marriage & Family, 61*(3), 813.

Leithwood, K., & Duke, D. (1998). A century's quest to understand school leadership. *Handbook of research on educational administration.* Washington, D.C.: American Educational Research Association.

Lincoln, Y.S., & Guba, E.G. (1985). *Naturalistic inquiry.* Beverly Hills, CA: Sage Publications.

Lord, R.G., & Day, D.V. (1998). Executive leadership and organizational performance: Suggestions for a new theory and methodology. *Journal of Management, 14,* 111–122.

Lord, R.G., & Maher, K.J. (2000). *Leadership and information processing: Linking perceptions and performance.* Boston: Unwin Hyman.

Lowe, K.B., Kroeck, K.G., & Sivasubramaniam, N. (1996). Effectiveness correlates of transformational and transactional leadership: A meta-analytic review of the MLQ literature. *Leadership Quarterly, 7,* 385–425.

Luke, J.S. (1991). New leadership requirements for public administration: From managerial to policy ethics. In J.S. Bowman (ed.), *Ethical frontiers in public management,* pp. 158–182. San Francisco: Jossey-Bass.

Luthar, S. (1991). Vulnerability and resilience: A study of high-risk adolescents. *Child Development, 62,* 600–616.

Maddux, J.E. (ed.). (1995). *Self-efficacy, adaptation, and adjustment: Theory, research and application.* New York: Plenum.

Masten, A.S., Best, K.M., & Garmezy, N. (1990). Resilience and development: Contributions from the study of children who overcome adversity. *Development and Psychopathology, 2,* 425–441.

Maxwell, J.A. (1996). *Qualitative research design: An interactive approach.* Thousand Oaks, CA: Sage Publications.

McCubbin, E.A., Thompson, E.A., Thompson, A.I., and Futrell, J.A. (1998). *Resilience in African American families.* Thousand Oaks, CA: Sage Publications.

McCubbin, H.I., McCubbin, M.A., & Thompson, A.I. (1992). Resiliency in families: The role of family schema and appraisal in family adaptation to rises. In T.H. Brubaker (ed.), *Family relations: Challenges for the future,* pp. 153–177. Newbury Park, CA: Sage Publications.

Merriam, S.B., & Associates. (2002). *Qualitative research in practice: Examples for discussion and analysis.* San Francisco: Jossey-Bass.

Miles, M.B., & Huberman, A.M. (1994). *Qualitative data analysis.* Thousand Oaks, CA: Sage Publications.

Moran, P.B., & Eckenrode, J. (1992). Protective personality characteristics among adolescent victims of maltreatment. *Child Abuse & Neglect, 16,* 743–754.

Morritz, C. (1989). *Current biography yearbook.* New York: H.W. Wilson.

Mosack, K. (2002). *Development and validation of the R-play: A resiliency measure for people living with HIV/AIDS.* Wooster: Ohio State University.

Mrazek, P.J., & Mrazek, D.A. (1987). Resilience in child maltreatment victims: A conceptual exploration. *Child Abuse & Neglect, 11,* 357–366.

Northhouse, P.G. (1997). Leadership: Theory and practice. Thousand Oaks, CA: Sage Publications.

Powell, K.C. (1998). *Developmental challenges and barriers: How senior executive women cope with difficult situations in their careers*. Amherst: University of Massachusetts.

Radke-Yarrow, M., & Brown, E. (1993). Resilience and vulnerability in children of multiple-risk families. *Development and Psychopathology, 5,* 581–592.

Radke-Yarrow, M., & Sherman, T. (1990). Hard growing: Children who survive. In J.E. Rolf and A.S. Masten (eds.), *Risk and protective factors in the development of psychopathology,* pp. 97–119. New York: Cambridge University Press.

Ramey, D.A. (1991). *Empowering leaders.* Kansas City, MO: Sheed & Ward.

Ramsey, J.L. & Blieszner, R. (1999) *Spiritual resiliency in older women: Models of strength for challenges through the life span.* Thousand Oaks: Sage Publications.

Richardson, G.E., Neiger, B.L., Jensen, S., & Kimpfer, K.L. (1990). The Resiliency Model. *Health Education, 21*(6), 33–39.

Rost, J.C. (1995). Leadership: A discussion about ethics. *Business Ethics Quarterly, 5*(1), 129–142.

Roth, A. (1949). *Current biography.* New York: H.W. Wilson.

Rutter, M. (1979). Protective factors in children's responses to stress and disadvantage. In M.W. Kent & J.E. Rolf (eds.), *Primary prevention of psychopathology,* vol. 3. Hanover, NH: University Press of New England.

Rutter, M. (1986). Meyerian psychobiology, personality development and the role of life experiences. *American Journal of Psychiatry, 143,* 1077–1087.

Rutter, M. (1987). Psychosocial resilience and protective mechanisms. *American Journal of Orthopsychiatry, 57,* 316–331.

Rutter, M. (1990). Psychosocial resilience and protective mechanisms. In J.W. Rolf, A.S. Masten, D. Cicchetti, K.H.

Neuchterlein, & S. Weintraub (eds.), *Risk and protective factors in the development of psychopathology*, pp. 181–214. Cambridge, England: Cambridge University Press.

Rutter, M. (1993). Resilience: Some conceptual considerations. *Journal of Adolescent Health, 14*(8), 626–631.

Rutter, M. & Taylor, E. (2002). *Child and Adolescent Psychiatry.* 4th ed. Oxford, England: Blackwell Publishers.

Schwandt, T.A. (2001). *Dictionary of qualitative inquiry* (2nd ed.). Thousand Oaks, CA: Sage.

Schwarzer, R. (ed.). (1992). *Self-efficacy: Thought control of action.* Washington, D.C.: Hemisphere.

Seidman, I.E. (1991). *Interviewing as qualitative research.* New York: Teachers College Press.

Senge, P. (1990). *The fifth discipline: The art and practice of the learning organization.* New York: Doubleday.

Sharmir, B., House, R.J., & Arthur, M.B. (1993). The motivational effects of charismatic leadership: A self-concept based theory. *Organizational science, 4,* 577–594.

Slocum, J., Ragan, C., & Casey, A. (2002). On death and dying: The corporate leadership capacity of CEO's *Organizational Dynamics,* 30(3), 269–81 (quoting Sorrel, 1991).

Smelser, N.J. (2001). Good leadership. In *International encyclopedia of the social & behavioral sciences,* vol. 13. New York: Elsevier.

Stogdill, R.M. (1948). Personal factors associated with leadership: A survey of the literature. *The Journal of Psychology,* 35–71.

Stogdill, R.M., & Coons, A.E. (eds.). (1957). *Leader behavior: Its description and measurement.* Wooster: Ohio State University.

Strauss, A., & Corbin, J. (1994). *Grounded theory methodology. Handbook of qualitative research.* Thousand Oaks, CA: Sage Publications.

Stroufe, L.A. (1997). Psychopathology as an outcome of development. *Development and Psychopathology, 9,* 251–268.

Tesch, R. (1990). *Qualitative research: Analysis types and software tools.* London: Falmer.

Thompson, C. (2000). *Current biography yearbook.* New York: H.W. Wilson.

Tichy, N.M., & Devanna, M.A., (1990). *The transformational leader: The key to global competitiveness.* New York: Wiley.

Valentine, L., & Feinauer, L. (1993). Resilience factors associated with female survivors of childhood sexual abuse. *American Journal of Family Therapy, 21,* 216–224.

Vecchio, R.P. (1987). Situational leadership theory: An examination of a prescriptive theory. *Journal of Applied Psychology,* (3), 444–445.

Walker, J.A. (1993). *Women's voices, women's lives: Understandings from women's twenty-four year correspondence.* University of Minnesota.

Werner, E. (1984, November). Resilient children. In *Young children,* pp. 68–72. Berlin: Duncker. & Humbolt Publisher.

Werner, E. (1993). Risk, resilience, and recovery: Perspectives from the Kauai longitudinal study. *Development and Psychopathology, 5,* 503–515. Berlin: Duncker & Humbolt Publisher.

Werner, E.E., & Smith, R. (1992). *Overcoming the odds: High-risk children from birth to adulthood.* Ithaca, NY: Cornell University Press.

Yukl, G. (1971). Toward a behavioral theory of leadership. *Organizational Behavior and Human Performance,* (3), 414–440.

Yukl, G.A. (1994). *Leadership in organizations* (3rd ed.). Englewood Cliffs, NJ: Prentice Hall.

About the Author

Motivational speaker and business consultant **Rev. Dr. Julia Baldwin** is also an ordained minister and the senior pastor at Sanctuary Ministries, a Christian church at Miami Lakes, Florida. Dr. Baldwin serves the Crisis Team for the Fire and Police Departments of Regions X and XI in Florida. The 113-year-old Trinity International University in Deerfield, Illinois, employed her as chief administrative officer for over six years. She led the university with her energetic character and formulated the university's first Prophecy Conference in the fall of 2002; she also conceived the first Business Conference in April of 2003, setting a new standard in fund-raising for the scholarship fund. Her doctoral research has led her to be invited as a distinguished lecturer at various universities in South Florida to discuss the newest topic in social science, resiliency theory. She is a graduate of Bernard M. Baruch College in New York City in the fields of business administration and finance. She has completed two master's degrees—one in religion at Trinity Evangelical Divinity School and the second in counseling psychology at Trinity International University. Her PhD work in education, with an emphasis in leadership and neuroscience, was completed at Barry University. Dr. Baldwin has launched a company called Endemic Motivation, Inc., which primarily deals with the topic addressed in her dissertation: "Resiliency Regarding Transformational Successful Women Leaders." She is currently the chairperson of the board for FLET University, where she has taught Christ-centered education in over twenty-two countries over the past thirty years. She also serves on the board of Miami Children's Hospital.